Key Stage Two English

Set A
Reading Booklet

This booklet contains:

The Fisherman
Summit Success for Intrepid Becky
Wild Camping

EHP27

CGP

Contents

The Fisherman

The Fisherman

The fisherman goes out at dawn
When every one's abed,
And from the bottom of the sea
Draws up his daily bread.

His life is strange; half on the shore
And half upon the sea —
Not quite a fish, and yet not quite
The same as you and me.

The fisherman has curious eyes;
They make you feel so queer,
As if they had seen many things
Of wonder and of fear.

They're like the sea on foggy days, —
Not gray, nor yet quite blue;
They're like the wondrous tales he tells
Not quite — yet maybe — true.

He knows so much of boats and tides,
Of winds and clouds and sky!
But when I tell of city things,
He sniffs and shuts one eye!

by Abbie Farwell Brown

Summit Success for Intrepid Becky

A librarian from Braunston has raised thousands of pounds for charity by successfully climbing Mont Blanc — the highest mountain in Western Europe.

By Gemma Ibbotson

Located in the Alps mountain range, Mont Blanc stands 4810m high and lies on the border between France and Italy. The permanently snow-covered summit gives the mountain its name, which means 'White Mountain' in English. Those tough enough to reach the top are greeted not only by breath-taking views, but also by dangerously low temperatures and ferocious winds.

Becky Arnott, 32, has recently returned from conquering this majestic mountain, and her feat has raised an astonishing £14 000 for charity. Becky has always enjoyed family

Becky on her way up to the summit of Mont Blanc, displaying her new skill with ice axes. Despite the difficulty of the ascent, she still had a smile on her face.

walks in the countryside, but climbing Mont Blanc was significantly harder than anything she had ever done previously. Before preparing for the challenge, she had never climbed higher than 1000m and she had never been on a mountain in the snow.

"My feet felt as though they were stuck in cement and I began to doubt that I could reach the top."

"I knew that it wasn't going to be a walk in the park," joked Becky. "I did some training on snowy mountains in Scotland and I hiked up two smaller mountains in the Alps to get used to the kinds of conditions I would face on Mont Blanc. I also had to learn how to walk on snow using crampons — spikes that fit to the bottom of your shoes — and an ice axe. This was tricky at first because it was much more technical than anything I was used to." Training complete, Becky set off on the gruelling two-day climb in early April.

"Becky had prepared well for the challenge, but even experienced mountaineers can find Mont Blanc a real struggle," explained Jean-Claude Durand, a mountain guide who accompanied Becky. "The climb is demanding and dangerous, and bad weather can turn a safe situation on its head within minutes. The high altitude is also a major problem because the higher you climb, the less oxygen there is, making it more difficult to breathe. Many people feel sick or dizzy as a result."

"I did find the altitude the hardest bit," agrees Becky. "I spent some time high in the mountains to let my body get accustomed to it, but all that climbing was tough going. As we tackled the final ascent, my lungs were burning, my feet felt as though they were stuck in cement and I began to doubt that I could reach the top. Thankfully, Jean-Claude kept encouraging me and I was spurred on by remembering the children at Holden Park. I cried tears of joy as we arrived on the summit."

"Access to the outdoors may reduce the children's recovery time."

It is the patients and staff at Holden Park Children's Hospital who will benefit from Becky's epic achievement. Becky's young nephew, Kamal, spent three months there last year and Becky was keen to give something back to the hospital. "Kamal received brilliant care at Holden Park and thanks to everyone there, he made a full recovery."

It's easy to see how Mont Blanc (the 'White Mountain') gets its name. The beautiful summit is permanently covered in snow.

"I was speaking to one of the nurses about wanting to help the hospital, and he mentioned that they were trying to raise some money to create a new garden space. That was the spark of inspiration for climbing Mont Blanc."

The staff at Holden Park are understandably delighted — not least because this is one of the largest amounts of money ever raised for the hospital by one person. In the garden which the money will help to create, the children will be able to play, sit outdoors and relax and even help the staff do some gardening to grow fruit, vegetables and flowers. Staff are hopeful that access to the outdoors may reduce the children's recovery time, as well as make their stay more enjoyable. "We'll be able to offer more activities to help the children build up strength and distract them from their problems," said a nurse from Holden Park.

"I never dreamt I'd raise so much money!"

Becky was taken aback by the amount of money that was donated. "People gave so generously," she said. "I'd like to thank everyone who donated — I never dreamt I'd raise so much money!"

Becky's challenging ascent certainly seems to have caught people's attention. "I can't even imagine trying to climb such a big mountain, so Becky's willingness to do this for charity made a real impression on me," said Patricia Ohuruogo, a local councillor who donated to Becky's cause. "I was thrilled when I heard that she had been successful, and it's wonderful that she has managed to raise so much money."

Following her fundraising success, Becky is planning to attempt more challenges to support Holden Park in the future. We wish her all the best in completing her next quest — whatever it may be!

Holden Park needs to raise more money — and you can help.

- Come to the cake sale at the hospital on 24th May from 11am to 2pm.
- Join in the 5km charity fun run around the Holden Park grounds on 15th June from 10am.

If you would like to get involved, contact Holden Park's Fundraising Manager, Sam Napier.

Wild Camping

It wasn't just spiders. People always presumed that it was just spiders, but Callum was scared of pretty much anything that moved. And now the day he'd been dreading had arrived: the day when creepy-crawlies would replace cushions and bugs would replace beds. He had never been camping before, but just the thought of it left Callum feeling queasy. Why would anyone choose to sleep in the woods rather than in a house?

"All ready, Cal?" shouted his dad enthusiastically. "The sun is shining, the tent is packed and the wilderness awaits us!"

Callum wished his dad wouldn't call it "the wilderness". It was bad enough that they were spending the weekend in the woods, without having to pretend that they were trekking to the Arctic. He slumped into the passenger seat of the car and prepared himself for the hour-long journey, which would probably be spent listening to his dad chattering away, as excited as a rabbit in a carrot field. At least it wasn't raining, he thought desperately, clutching onto the only positive he could think of.

It was his sister's hamster that had done it, almost two years ago. Callum had never really been interested in animals, but after the rest of the family had excitedly cuddled and cooed over the new pet, it was passed to him. He'd hoped to hold it for a few seconds, give it a stroke and then give it back, but the furry critter had other ideas. It scuttled up his arm, ran across his chest and jumped down into his lap. Panicked by the hamster's frenzied movement, Callum tried to grab it, but it responded by biting him hard on the finger. The bite only hurt a little bit, but Callum had vowed that he would never hold an animal ever again.

The first fat droplets of rain splashed onto the forest floor just as Callum and his dad got the campfire going. "Better get these sausages on," chirped Dad.

Callum's face was as colourless as the slate grey sky, and every rustling leaf, crunching twig and cooing pigeon made him flinch. The towering regiments of trees that surrounded their camp appeared cold and threatening to Callum, and he felt a long way from home. "There's nothing out here that will bother us, Cal. It's great being surrounded by nature."

Callum wanted to believe him, but he was suspicious of the forest's hidden army of birds, bugs and beasts and was keen to avoid meeting them. Even watching the dancing flames of the campfire and eating the sausages – normally his favourite – brought him little comfort.

"What was that?" exclaimed Callum. Something had sped behind the campfire and disappeared into the undergrowth. Squirrel? Fox? Wolf? His mind flicked through an imaginary picture book of woodland creatures. Whatever it was, he hadn't seen it properly and couldn't tell how big it was – it had just been a flash of grey in the dusky light. "Dad, did you see that?"

"I didn't see anything," replied Dad. "It was probably just a spark from the fire." But Callum knew he'd seen something, and he didn't like the fact that it had been so close.

It was getting dark now, and as night fell the natural orchestra of the forest struck up a different, more sinister tune. The pattering of the rain had eventually subsided, leaving behind only the sounds of the forest which swirled around Callum. Another noise: a persistent rustling. This time much closer.

"Dad, can you hear that?" asked Callum. "It sounds as though there is something in the tent."

Dad looked up from his book and chuckled gently, "It's just the wind blowing some leaves around – don't worry, Cal."

Callum smiled nervously and tried to ignore the noise, but he knew it was there. What was it? Rat? Badger? Snake?

Dad let out a loud, exaggerated yawn and suggested that they head to bed for the night. Callum was sure that he wouldn't sleep, but there were no obvious signs of any unwelcome visitors in the tent. He unrolled his sleeping bag, tucked himself inside it and listened in the darkness to the clumsy rustling of his dad doing the same.

"Night, Cal," said Dad.

"Night, Dad," replied Cal.

"Get out! Hey! Ouch!" Panic pulsed through Callum's veins as he was startled by his dad's frantic shouting. "Arrgghh! No! Ow!" Bewildered, Callum stretched his trembling hand across to where his bedside lamp would be, but found only the smooth canvas of the tent lining and quickly remembered where he was. He dived out of his sleeping bag to find his torch, accompanied by a soundtrack of his dad's grunting and a shrill squealing that he presumed was coming from his dad's attacker. After what felt like hours of scrabbling around, Callum finally recovered his torch and quickly shone it across the tent, fearful of what its yellowish light would reveal.

Now illuminated was his dad, wrestling with his sleeping bag as if it were a slippery sea monster. It took a few more seconds for Callum's eyes to fall upon the terrible creature that his dad was trying to discover and defeat. There, sitting next to his dad's inflatable pillow, with panicked wide eyes and twitching ears, was a fluffy grey rabbit. Callum was simultaneously relieved that it was only a rabbit and terrified that the creature was so close, but at that moment he noticed that his dad – still writhing in his sleeping bag – was about to come toppling down on top of it. Without thinking, he thrust his arms forward and grabbed the rabbit.

Thud. Dad and his sleeping bag crashed onto the floor. With a groan, he slowly picked himself up and looked sheepishly towards Callum. To his surprise, he found his son clutching a small grey rabbit. Without saying anything, Callum edged towards the entrance of the tent, opened the zip, and gently ushered the rabbit out into the woods.

Key Stage Two English

Set A
Reading

Answer Booklet
1 hour

First name	
Middle name	
Last name	
School	

Date of birth	Day		Month		Year	

Total marks

Instructions

This booklet tests your **reading comprehension**. The test has different question types, which you will need to answer in different ways. Each question has a space for you to give your answer. This will show you the type of answer to give:

Short-answer questions: you'll get one or two lines to write your answer on, so just write a word, a short phrase or a single sentence.

Long-answer questions: you'll be given several lines to write your answer on. You should use full sentences and explain your answer in more detail, giving reasons for your opinion or using quotations from the reading text.

Other types of answer: for some questions, you do not have to write anything. Instead, you might have to tick the correct box, circle the right answer or draw lines to match up words. Read the questions carefully and they'll tell you what to do.

The maximum number of marks available is written next to each question.

Do not start until your teacher tells you to. Start on page 3 and work through the booklet until you are told to stop.

Read one text and answer the questions on it before moving on to the next text. Use your reading booklet whenever you need to.

When a question mentions a particular page of the reading booklet, look at that page to help you write your answer.

You will have **1 hour** to answer all the questions.

SECTION 1

> **These questions are about *The Fisherman***

1 When does the fisherman leave to go fishing each day?

_____

2 *When every one's abed*

What does the word *abed* mean in the line above?

Tick **one** box.

out of bed ☐

at work ☐

at home ☐

in bed ☐

3 *And from the bottom of the sea*
Draws up his daily bread.

Explain what the fisherman's *daily bread* is.

_____

_____

KS2 English / Set A / Reading Answer Booklet

The Fisherman

4 *Not quite a fish, and yet not quite*
The same as you and me.

According to the poem, why is the fisherman like this?

_____

_____

1 mark

5 *The fisherman has curious eyes;*
They make you feel so queer

What does the word *queer* mean in the lines above?

Tick **one** box.

seasick ☐

happy ☐

odd ☐

suspicious ☐

1 mark

6 Look at the verse that begins *They're like the sea...*

Find and **copy one** word meaning amazing.

_____

1 mark

7 List **four** things from the poem that the fisherman could tell you about.

1. _____

2. _____

3. _____

4. _____

2 marks

8 What does the line *He sniffs and shuts one eye!* tell you about how the fisherman feels about city things?

_____

_____

1 mark

9 What does the poem make the reader think about the fisherman?

Explain your answer using examples from the poem.

_____

_____

_____

_____

_____

2 marks

SECTION 2

> **These questions are about**
> *Summit Success for Intrepid Becky*

10 What job does Becky do?

_____

1 mark

11 Look at the paragraph on page 5 which begins *Located in the Alps...*

Find and **copy** a word from this paragraph which shows that the wind is strong on the summit of Mont Blanc.

_____

1 mark

12 Read each sentence and tick **one** box to show whether it is **true** or **false**.

	True	False
Mont Blanc is the highest mountain in Western Europe.	☐	☐
Mont Blanc is on the border between France and Switzerland.	☐	☐
Mont Blanc's summit is permanently covered in snow.	☐	☐
Becky is 33 years old.	☐	☐

1 mark

13 Look at the text on page 5. Give **two** things Becky did during her training to climb Mont Blanc which she had never done before.

1. _____

2. _____

1 mark

14 Look at the text on page 6. What are crampons?

_____

_____

1 mark

15 *...bad weather can turn a safe situation on its head within minutes.*

What does the phrase *turn a safe situation on its head* mean in the sentence above?

_____

_____

1 mark

16 *The high altitude is also a major problem...*

Give **two** effects that high altitude can have on climbers.

1. _____

2. _____

1 mark

17 How can you tell that Becky's legs were tired when she was near the summit?

_____

_____

1 mark

18 *...I began to doubt that I could reach the top.*

Give **one** thing that helped Becky to reach the top when she began to doubt herself.

_____

1 mark

19 Climbing Mont Blanc is thought to be very difficult.

Find and **copy three** words from the text on page 6 which support this view.

1. _____

2. _____

3. _____

2 marks

20 Look at the paragraph that begins *It is the patients and staff...*

How can you tell that the writer, Gemma Ibbotson, thinks that Becky's climb was impressive?

_____

_____

1 mark

21 Read each sentence and tick **one** box to show whether it is a **fact** or an **opinion**.

	Fact	Opinion
Becky raised an astonishing amount of money.	☐	☐
Becky did some training before climbing Mont Blanc.	☐	☐
Holden Park is a children's hospital.	☐	☐
Kamal received brilliant care at the hospital.	☐	☐

1 mark

22 Look at the paragraph beginning *Becky's challenging ascent...*

Draw lines to match each word on the left to a word on the right which could replace it in the text.

challenging	impact
willingness	elated
impression	demanding
thrilled	readiness

2 marks

23 How can you tell that Patricia Ohuruogo supports what Becky has done?
Use evidence from the text to support your answer.

_____

_____

_____

_____

2 marks

24 How does the final page of the article encourage the reader
to raise money for Holden Park? Give **two** ways.

_____

_____

_____

_____

2 marks

SECTION 3

> **These questions are about *Wild Camping***

25 Choose the best word or group of words to fit the sentences below, and circle your choice.

a) Callum and his dad are going camping

by a river.	in the woods.	on a hillside.	in a field.

1 mark

b) In the second paragraph, Callum's dad shouts

angrily.	impatiently.	excitedly.	anxiously.

1 mark

c) Callum's fear of holding animals was started by

a hamster.	a squirrel.	a spider.	a snake.

1 mark

d) It starts to rain while Callum and his dad are

travelling.	sleeping.	eating sausages.	lighting the fire.

1 mark

Wild Camping

26 Look at the paragraph that begins *Callum wished his dad...*

How does this paragraph suggest that Callum is feeling annoyed?

_____

1 mark

27 Look at the paragraph that begins *It was his sister's...*

How can you tell that the rest of Callum's family all like animals?

_____

1 mark

28 *Panicked by the hamster's frenzied movement...*

Which of the following words has a similar meaning to *frenzied*?

Tick **one** box.

joyful ☐

frightening ☐

frantic ☐

awkward ☐

1 mark

29 Give **two** things that the hamster does to Callum.

1. _____

2. _____

1 mark

30 Look at the paragraph that begins *Callum's face was as colourless as...*

Give **two** things from this paragraph that scare Callum.

1. _____

2. _____   1 mark

31 *...the forest's hidden army of birds, bugs and beasts...*

What does the word *army* tell you about what Callum thinks about the birds, bugs and beasts in the forest?

_____   1 mark

32 Look at the last three paragraphs on page 9 from *"What was that?"* to *This time much closer.*

Tick the statement that is the best summary of what happens in these paragraphs.

Tick **one** box.

Darkness falls in the forest.   ☐

Callum sees an animal.   ☐

Callum sees and hears things that scare him.   ☐

Callum hears a rustling noise.   ☐   1 mark

33 **Find** and **copy** a word from page 10 which shows that Callum is confused.

_____   1 mark

34 Callum's dad *chuckled gently* (page 10).

Why does he do this?

_____

_____ 1 mark

35 a) The characters feel different emotions throughout the story.

Find and **copy** the words on page 10 that show where Callum's dad's emotions change.

_____ 1 mark

b) How do Callum's dad's emotions change?

_____

_____ 1 mark

36 Look at the text on page 11.

Explain what these two paragraphs show about Callum's personality. Use evidence from the text to support your answer.

_____

_____

_____

_____

_____ 2 marks

37 Do you think Callum will still be scared of animals after the trip?
Tick **one** box.

Yes ☐   No ☐   Maybe ☐

Explain your answer using evidence from the text.

_____

_____

_____

_____

_____

_____

_____

3 marks

END OF TEST

[Blank Page]

EHP27U

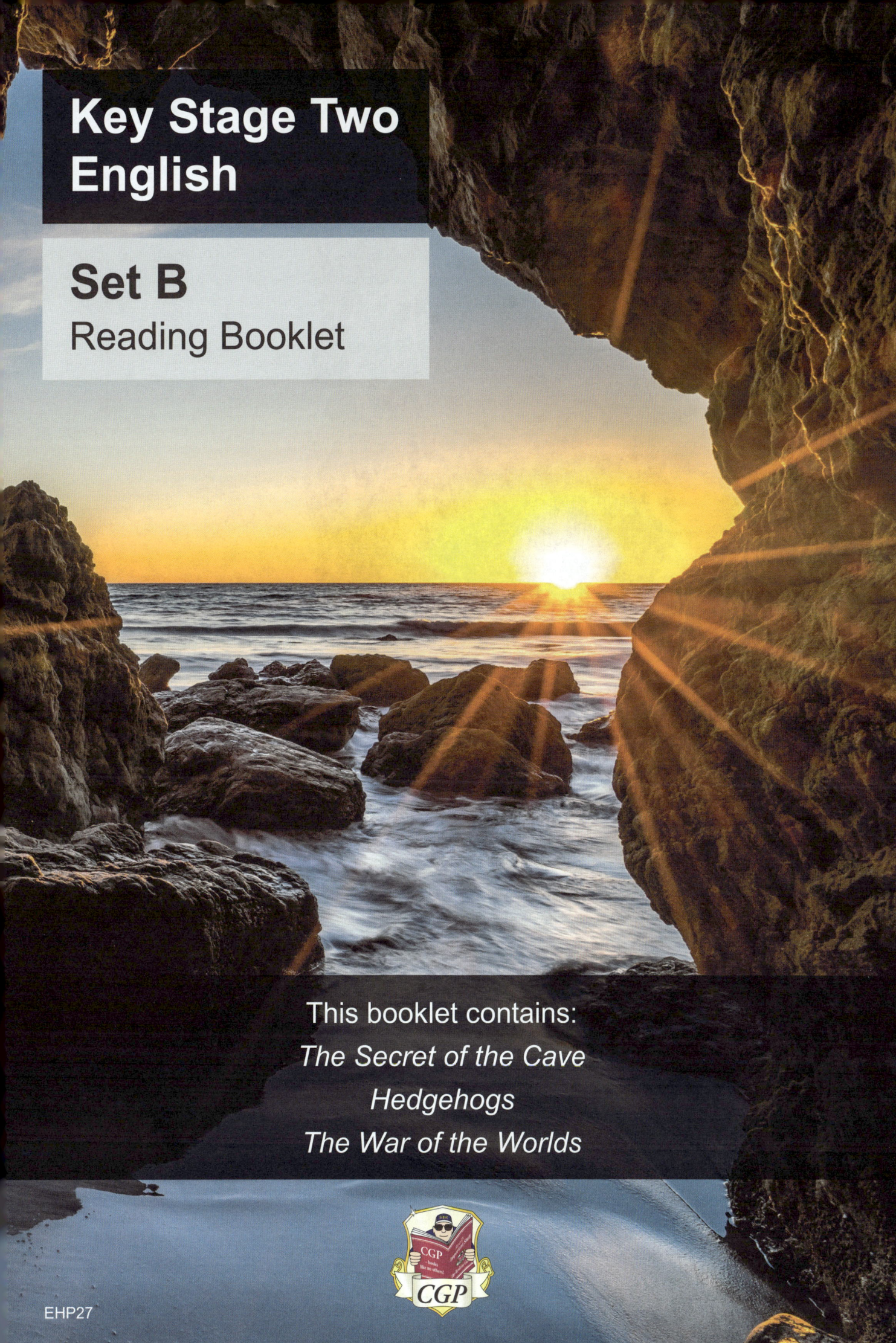

Key Stage Two English

Set B
Reading Booklet

This booklet contains:
The Secret of the Cave
Hedgehogs
The War of the Worlds

EHP27

Contents

KS2 English / Set B / Reading Booklet

The Secret of the Cave

The sun's rays were beating down on the beach as Jack and Ben hurried towards the edge of the water, strapping on their snorkels and masks as they went. They swam out into the sea and submerged their masked faces in the clear, deep water, trying to spot some ocean wildlife.

Swimming around slowly, Jack stared in awe as a green turtle darted past him and swarms of colourful fish floated around like multi-coloured clouds. A coral reef stretched like a forest across the ocean floor that was now out of reach of their feet. All Jack could hear with his ears submerged in the water was the steady rhythm of his slow, deep breathing.

He was so lost in his thoughts that he jerked around in fright when he felt a tap on his shoulder. Ben was pointing with one hand towards the sky. They resurfaced, pulling the snorkels from their mouths.

"Staring at fish is getting boring," said Ben. "We should go look in there." He nodded towards an outcrop of rock a short distance away. In the wall of rock, there was a large crack that led into a cave. It looked like the jaws of a wild animal, ready to swallow them whole.

"It might be dangerous," said Jack, nervously eyeing the rock's jagged edges and the waves thrashing up against it. Ben seemed not to have heard him though, as he had already started swimming towards the rock. After hesitating for a moment, Jack followed.

As they got closer to the rock, the waves buffeted Jack and Ben from side to side. Jack watched as Ben, who was a much stronger swimmer, disappeared into the mouth of the cave. Panic began to rise in his chest, and he had to use all of his strength to drag his arms and legs through the water and propel his body forward.

Finally, Jack reached the cave, and was relieved to find that the water was much calmer inside. When he got further in, he saw Ben crouching on a rocky ledge that stuck out from beneath the water, examining what appeared to be a large wooden crate.

"What's that?" asked Jack, scrambling onto the ledge and walking over to his brother.

Ben looked at him without saying a word, his eyes wide. He then opened the lid of the crate fully so that Jack could see inside.

An incredible sight met Jack's eyes — the crate contained thousands of priceless gold coins. The brothers looked at each other, laughing in disbelief. Still kneeling beside the crate, they debated where it might have come from, and wondered if it had been lost at sea and washed into the cave by the waves. The excitement building in his voice, Jack pointed out that they might be rewarded if they returned the crate to its owner.

"We'll need to go and fetch our dinghy, and then come back for it," said Ben. "There's no way we can stay afloat if we carry it."

They lowered themselves back into the water and began to swim towards the entrance of the cave. But as they neared the cave's mouth, chatting enthusiastically about their adventure, a gruff voice interrupted their conversation. Looking up, they found their path blocked by a boat that towered over them, and on the boat's deck stood several men, scowling down at them.

Hedgehogs

What are Hedgehogs?

Hedgehogs are a type of small mammal found in Europe, Asia, Africa and New Zealand. There are various different species of hedgehog, but the type we see in the UK is known as the European Hedgehog. The name 'hedgehog' is derived from the way the animal searches for food: they forage around in hedges while making grunting pig-like noises.

Hedgehogs are easily recognisable from the sharp quills that cover their back and head. Although this may sound sinister, the purpose of the quills is actually protection: if hedgehogs feel threatened, they can curl up into a spiky ball, making it painful for predators that try to eat them. Their face, chest, stomach, neck and legs are covered in fur, and they have small ears and a tail as well as a long snout that they use to rummage around for food. When they look for food, they predominantly use their senses of smell and hearing, as their eyesight is relatively poor.

Hedgehog Hibernation

The creatures that make up the diet of a hedgehog become more scarce when the temperature drops, so hedgehogs that live in countries with frigid winters need to hibernate to help them survive without food. This means they go into a type of long, deep sleep where their metabolism (bodily functions, such as their heart rate) slows down. The small amount of energy they need to survive is provided by the surplus fat that they build up through the summer, when they eagerly gorge themselves on food.

Hedgehogs usually hibernate between November and March, so it is something of a rarity for humans to see one out in the open during this time of the year. Even during milder months, sightings of hedgehogs remain fairly uncommon: they are mainly nocturnal animals, so they sleep during the day and wake up at night to search for food.

Attracting Hedgehogs

Hedgehogs are often referred to as the 'gardener's friend' because they will happily feast upon a variety of pests (such as slugs and caterpillars) that can wreak havoc on gardeners' plants. But this doesn't mean that you should go out in search of a hedgehog to keep in your garden — they are wild animals, and they need  to roam over a wide area in order to get a sufficient amount of food. You can, though, do a few things to make your garden a more inviting place for hedgehogs, so that they will want to come and visit.

> Have a look at the next page to see how you can make your garden more hedgehog friendly.

Helping Out Hedgehogs

1. Put Out Food and Water

Although hedgehogs are perfectly capable of finding their own food, this doesn't mean they won't eat other things they are offered to supplement their diet. Some examples of things you could put out are certain types of cat or dog foods, boiled eggs, or even special hedgehog food. Make sure you don't give bread to a hedgehog, and never offer them cows' milk, as this can give them stomach problems and may even be fatal. If you're worried that other, larger animals might beat the hedgehogs to the punch, you could put the food in a sealed container and cut out a hole that only a hedgehog would be able to fit through.

2. Make Sure They Can Get In

Hedgehogs can negotiate hedges, but they find it hard to get over walls and fences, so you need to make things easy for them. You could cut a small hole in your fence for them to fit through, or have a fence with gaps between the panels. You could even encourage your neighbours to follow your good example, creating a network of gardens for hedgehogs to explore.

3. Leave an Overgrown Area

Hedgehogs can't make a home out of a neatly trimmed lawn, but if you have long grass, branches and twigs in your garden, they might come along to take them for their nests, or even sleep or hibernate amongst them.

4. Make your Garden Safe

If you're hoping a hedgehog will stop off in your garden, it's essential that you make it a safe place for them. A garden containing litter could be a deathtrap for hedgehogs, so make sure you keep your garden tidy and free of things that could ensnare them. If you have a pond, make sure that they can't fall in, or that if they do, they can easily escape. Although hedgehogs can swim, they could drown if they get stuck in the water. Also, if you do any gardening, make sure you check any long grass for hedgehogs before using sharp or bladed tools, such as lawn mowers.

The War of the Worlds

This is an extract from *The War of the Worlds* by H.G. Wells, written and set in the late 19th century. A series of explosions have been observed on the surface of Mars, but no one knows what is causing them. In this extract, an unnamed narrator recounts what happened some time later, as a shooting star falls to Earth...

Then came the night of the first falling star. It was seen early in the morning, rushing over Winchester eastward, a line of flame high in the atmosphere. Hundreds must have seen it, and taken it for an ordinary falling star. Albin described it as leaving a greenish streak behind it that glowed for some seconds. Denning, our greatest authority on meteorites*, stated that the height of its first appearance was about ninety or one hundred miles. It seemed to him that it fell to earth about one hundred miles east of him.

I was at home at that hour and writing in my study; and although my French windows face towards Ottershaw and the blind was up (for I loved in those days to look up at the night sky), I saw nothing of it. Yet this strangest of all things that ever came to earth from outer space must have fallen while I was sitting there, visible to me had I only looked up as it passed. Some of those who saw its flight say it travelled with a hissing sound. I myself heard nothing of that. Many people in Berkshire, Surrey, and Middlesex must have seen the fall of it, and, at most, have thought that another meteorite had descended. No one seems to have troubled to look for the fallen mass that night.

* meteorites = rocks that have fallen to earth from space

But very early in the morning poor Ogilvy, who had seen the shooting star and who was persuaded that a meteorite lay somewhere on the common between Horsell, Ottershaw, and Woking, rose early with the idea of finding it. Find it he did, soon after dawn, and not far from the sand pits. An enormous hole had been made by the impact of the projectile*, and the sand and gravel had been flung violently in every direction over the heath, forming heaps visible a mile and a half away. The heather was on fire eastward, and a thin blue smoke rose against the dawn.

The Thing itself lay almost entirely buried in sand, amidst the scattered splinters of a fir tree it had shivered to fragments in its descent. The uncovered part had the appearance of a huge cylinder, caked over and its outline softened by a thick scaly dun-coloured incrustation. It had a diameter of about thirty yards. He approached the mass, surprised at the size and more so at the shape, since most meteorites are rounded more or less completely. It was, however, still so hot from its flight through the air as to forbid his near approach. A stirring noise within its cylinder he ascribed to the unequal cooling of its surface; for at that time it had not occurred to him that it might be hollow.

He remained standing at the edge of the pit that the Thing had made for itself, staring at its strange appearance, astonished chiefly at its unusual shape and colour, and dimly perceiving even then some evidence of design* in its arrival. The early morning was wonderfully still, and the sun, just clearing the pine trees towards Weybridge, was already warm. He did not remember hearing any birds that morning, there was certainly no breeze stirring, and the only sounds were the faint movements from within the cindery cylinder. He was all alone on the common.

* projectile = an object that has been moved through the air with force
* design = thought, intent

Then suddenly he noticed with a start that some of the grey clinker, the ashy incrustation that covered the meteorite, was falling off the circular edge of the end. It was dropping off in flakes and raining down upon the sand. A large piece suddenly came off and fell with a sharp noise that brought his heart into his mouth.

For a minute he scarcely realised what this meant, and, although the heat was excessive, he clambered down into the pit close to the bulk to see the Thing more clearly. He fancied even then that the cooling of the body might account for this, but what disturbed that idea was the fact that the ash was falling only from the end of the cylinder.

And then he perceived that, very slowly, the circular top of the cylinder was rotating on its body. It was such a gradual movement that he discovered it only through noticing that a black mark that had been near him five minutes ago was now at the other side of the circumference. Even then he scarcely understood what this indicated, until he heard a muffled grating sound and saw the black mark jerk forward an inch or so. Then the thing came upon him in a flash. The cylinder was artificial — hollow — with an end that screwed out! Something within the cylinder was unscrewing the top!

Key Stage Two English

Set B
Reading

Answer Booklet
1 hour

First name	
Middle name	
Last name	
School	

Date of birth	Day		Month		Year	

Total marks

This booklet tests your **reading comprehension**. The test has different question types, which you will need to answer in different ways. Each question has a space for you to give your answer. This will show you the type of answer to give:

Short-answer questions: you'll get one or two lines to write your answer on, so just write a word, a short phrase or a single sentence.

Long-answer questions: you'll be given several lines to write your answer on. You should use full sentences and explain your answer in more detail, giving reasons for your opinion or using quotations from the reading text.

Other types of answer: for some questions, you do not have to write anything. Instead, you might have to tick the correct box, circle the right answer or draw lines to match up words. Read the questions carefully and they'll tell you what to do.

The maximum number of marks available is written next to each question.

Do not start until your teacher tells you to. Start on page 3 and work through the booklet until you are told to stop.

Read one text and answer the questions on it before moving on to the next text. Use your reading booklet whenever you need to.

When a question mentions a particular page of the reading booklet, look at that page to help you write your answer.

You will have **1 hour** to answer all the questions.

SECTION 1

> ## These questions are about *The Secret of the Cave*

1 Choose the best word or group of words to fit the sentences below, and circle your choice.

a) Jack and Ben approach the sea

| quickly. | fearfully. | carefully. | slowly. |

_____
1 mark

b) When they are in the cave, they find a crate full of

| silver. | coins. | diamonds. | jewellery. |

_____
1 mark

c) They see the men on the boat when they are

| going to get their dinghy. | swimming underwater. | on the beach. | opening the crate. |

_____
1 mark

2 Look at the paragraph that begins *Swimming around...*

Find and **copy one** word meaning large groups.

_____

_____
1 mark

3 Write down **three** things that Jack sees under the water.

1. _____

2. _____

3. _____

2 marks

4 What does Ben do to get Jack's attention?

_____

1 mark

5 *It looked like the jaws of a wild animal, ready to swallow them whole.*

What impression does this give you of the cave?

_____

_____

1 mark

6 Look at the last paragraph on page 4.

How can you tell that Jack is reluctant to go to the cave?
Give **two** points.

1. _____

2. _____   2 marks

7 Why was Ben able to get to the cave before Jack?

_____   1 mark

8 How can you tell that Ben is shocked about what is in the crate?
Give **two** points.

1. _____

2. _____   2 marks

9 How do Jack and Ben think the crate got into the cave?

_____

1 mark

10 Why might they be rewarded if they return the crate to its owner?

_____

1 mark

11 Read each sentence and tick **one** box to show whether it is **true** or **false**.

	True	False
The sea is rough inside the cave.	☐	☐
Ben suggests carrying the crate to the beach in a dinghy.	☐	☐
The crate is on a rocky ledge.	☐	☐
Jack wants to swim back to the beach with the crate.	☐	☐

1 mark

12 How do you know that the men on the boat are angry with Jack and Ben?

_____

_____

1 mark

SECTION 2

These questions are about *Hedgehogs*

---

13 How did hedgehogs get their name?
Tick **two** boxes.

Tick **two** boxes.

They are small mammals. ☐

They are found all over the world. ☐

They forage around in hedges. ☐

They have sharp quills on their back and head. ☐

They make grunting, pig-like noises. ☐

1 mark

---

14 *Hedgehogs are easily recognisable from the sharp quills...*

Which of the following words has a similar meaning to *recognisable*?

Tick **one** box.

apparent ☐

clear ☐

identifiable ☐

obvious ☐

1 mark

KS2 English / Set B / Reading Answer Booklet

Hedgehogs

15 What do hedgehogs do when they feel threatened?

_____

1 mark

16 Why don't hedgehogs eat very much during winter?
Give **two** reasons.

1. _____

2. _____

2 marks

17 ...*when they eagerly gorge themselves on food.*

What does the phrase *eagerly gorge themselves* tell you
about how hedgehogs eat in the summer?

_____

1 mark

18 Using information from the text, explain why sightings of hedgehogs are rare.

_____

_____

_____

_____

2 marks

19 According to the text, why might someone want a hedgehog to visit their garden?

_____

_____ 1 mark

20 Give **one** reason from the text that explains why you shouldn't keep a hedgehog in your garden.

_____

_____ 1 mark

21 Read each sentence and tick **one** box to show whether it is **true** or **false**.

	True	False
There is only one species of hedgehog in the world.	☐	☐
There is less food available for hedgehogs in winter.	☐	☐
You should give cows' milk to hedgehogs.	☐	☐
Hedgehogs can get through hedges.	☐	☐

1 mark

22 Do you think people should put out food for hedgehogs?
Tick **one** box.

Yes ☐   No ☐   Maybe ☐

Explain your answer using information from the text.

_____

_____

_____

_____

2 marks

23 *You could even encourage your neighbours to follow your good example...*

What does the phrase *follow your good example* mean in the sentence above?

_____

1 mark

24 Why might leaving long grass, branches and twigs
in a garden attract hedgehogs? Give **two** reasons.

1. _____

2. _____

1 mark

25 Why should you check long grass for hedgehogs before using a lawn mower?

_____

_____

1 mark

> ### These questions are about *The War of the Worlds*

26 Look at the paragraph that begins *Then came the night...*

What does the word *rushing* suggest about the meteorite?

_____

_____

1 mark

27 In what direction was the meteorite travelling?

_____

1 mark

28 Look at the paragraph that begins *Then came the night...*

Find and **copy one** word meaning expert.

_____

1 mark

29 Give **two** reasons why the narrator is surprised that
he did not see the meteorite fall to Earth.

1. _____

2. _____

1 mark

30 Where does Ogilvy think the meteorite has landed?

Tick **one** box.

towards Weybridge ☐

Winchester ☐

Berkshire, Surrey or Middlesex ☐

between Horsell, Ottershaw and Woking ☐

1 mark

31 Look at the paragraph that begins *But very early in the morning...*

Give **two** effects of the impact of the meteorite.

1. _____

2. _____

1 mark

32 Look at the paragraph that begins *The Thing itself lay...*

How can you tell that the Thing landed with a lot of force?

_____

_____

1 mark

33 Look at the paragraph that begins *The Thing itself lay...*

Draw lines to match each word on the left to a word on the right which could replace it in the text.

buried		exposed

amidst		prevent

uncovered		among

forbid		embedded

2 marks

34 Look at the paragraph that begins *He remained standing...*

How does this paragraph suggest that the Thing is not a natural meteorite?

_____

_____

1 mark

35 **Find** and **copy one** phrase or sentence that shows the moment where Ogilvy realises why the top of the cylinder is moving.

_____

1 mark

36 How do you think Ogilvy feels as he investigates the Thing?

Explain your answer using evidence from the text.

_____

_____

_____

_____

_____

_____

3 marks

37 Some of the paragraphs in the text have been summarised below.
Put them in the order they appear in the text.
The first one has been done for you.

Ogilvy climbs down into the pit. ☐

A meteorite falls to Earth. ☐ 1

A description of the meteorite's appearance. ☐

The meteorite is found. ☐

Ogilvy realises the truth. ☐

Ash is falling off the meteorite. ☐

1 mark

38 What do you think **happens next** in the story?

Explain your answer using information from the text.

_____

_____

_____

_____

2 marks

END OF TEST

[Blank Page]

Key Stage Two English

Set A
Grammar, Punctuation and Spelling

Paper 1: Questions
45 minutes

First name	
Middle name	
Last name	
School	

Date of birth	Day		Month		Year	

Paper 2, the spelling task, is a pull-out section in the middle of the booklet.

Total marks

Exam Set EHP27

[Blank Page]

Instructions

This booklet tests your **grammar**, **vocabulary** and **punctuation**. The test has different question types, which you will need to answer in different ways. Each question has a space for you to give your answer. This will show you the type of answer to give:

Multiple-choice answers: you can answer these questions without writing any words. You might have to tick a box, circle a word or draw lines between different words. Read the instructions for each question carefully, as they will tell you what to do.

Short answers: these questions have a line or a box for your answer. This shows that you need to write something. It could be a word, a short phrase or a sentence.

There is a mark box next to each question. It tells you the maximum number of marks for that question.

Do not start until your teacher tells you to. Once you have started the test, work through the booklet until you are told to stop.

You will have 45 minutes to answer all the questions.

1 Read the sentence below.
Which **word class** does the word '**reply**' belong to?

Ben wanted to **reply** to the letter.

Tick **one** box.

noun ☐

verb ☐

adjective ☐

adverb ☐

1 mark

2 The sentence below is missing a **question mark**.
Tick **one** box to show where the question mark should go.

"We're going to the restaurant, aren't we" asked Nikhil.

 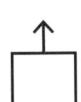 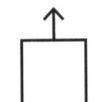

1 mark

3 Read the options below.
Tick the option which is punctuated correctly.

Tick **one** box.

"What an amazing house that is." gasped Yasmin? ☐

"What an amazing house that is!" gasped Yasmin. ☐

"What an amazing house that is" gasped Yasmin. ☐

"What an amazing house that is?" gasped Yasmin. ☐

1 mark

4 Underline the **adverbial** in the sentence below.

After lunch, I had a piece of chocolate cake.

1 mark

5 Read the sentences below. In the box, write the **expanded form** of the words that are underlined.

We <u>can't</u> find the baking powder or the sugar.
↓

You <u>shouldn't</u> leave your shoes on in the house.
↓

1 mark

6 Read the sentence below.
Tick the word that is an **adverb**.

The village was quite easy to find when we used our map.

Tick **one** box.

village ☐

easy ☐

quite ☐

used ☐

1 mark

7 Read the sentences below.
Choose a **conjunction** from the box to fill each gap and write it on the line.
You can only use each conjunction **once**.

| or | after | although |

He said that, _____ it is raining, we can go for a walk _____

we have eaten. I'd rather stay inside _____ go to the swimming pool.

1 mark

8 Read the sentence below and circle the word or words that make it a **question**.

I asked him to take the dog for a long walk, didn't I?

1 mark

9 Read the sentences below.
Tick the **two** sentences which are **statements**.

Tick **two** boxes.

When we get home, go to bed. ☐

We should try to get tickets early. ☐

I told you to turn left at the end of the road. ☐

We're not going to the top of the tower, are we? ☐

1 mark

10 Tick **one** box to show where the **semi-colon** should go in this sentence.

My auntie has bought a new house it's much bigger than her old one.

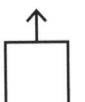 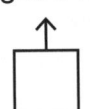 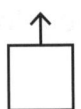

_____
1 mark

11 Look at the table below. Change the question into a **command**.
Write the command in the right-hand column.

Question	Command
Could you unlock the gate?	

_____
1 mark

12 Read the sentence below.
Write what Andrew needs to pack as a list of bullet points below.
Make sure you use correct punctuation.

Andrew needs to pack jeans, toothpaste, pyjamas and socks for his trip.

For his trip, Andrew needs to pack:

- _____

- _____

- _____

- _____

1 mark

13 Read the sentences below.
Circle the word that includes an **apostrophe** for **possession**.

I'm teaching myself to play the guitar using my mum's old guitar.

It's quite difficult because it has a string missing.

1 mark

14 Read the sentence below.
Write the **name** of the punctuation mark that appears between the words coasters and Emma on the line.

I like really scary roller coasters; Emma hates them.

_____

1 mark

15 Draw a line to match each word with its **synonym**.
You can only use each synonym **once**.

Word	Synonym
suitable	difficult
challenging	obvious
apparent	appropriate
tedious	unexciting

1 mark

16 Read the sentences below.
Circle all of the **adjectives**.

Sarah's new puppy is very playful. It loves to chew its favourite toy.

17 Read the sentences below.
Tick **one** box to show which sentence means dinner is **most likely** to be ready soon.

Tick **one** box.

Dinner might be ready soon. ☐

Dinner will be ready soon. ☐

Dinner should be ready soon. ☐

Dinner could be ready soon. ☐

1 mark

18 Underline the **object** in each of these sentences.

Chris congratulated his team after the rounders game.

This morning, I ate two apples.

We bought a television at the supermarket.

1 mark

19 Draw lines to match each sentence with the correct **function**.
Each function box should only be used **once**.

Sentence		Function
Plan the journey carefully		statement
Will the journey be very long		question
The journey will last around six hours		command
What a long journey we have had		exclamation

1 mark

20 Read the sentences below. Circle the correct word in brackets to complete each sentence using **Standard English**.

I **(was / were)** about to start reading a new book.

We haven't had **(anything / nothing)** to eat since lunchtime.

I wore the coat **(that / what)** my grandma bought for me.

1 mark

21 Tick the box below the part of the sentence that is a **relative clause**.

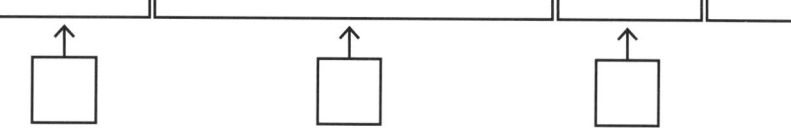

Adam's suit which his mother bought him is hanging at the back of his wardrobe.

1 mark

22 Read the passage below. Write an **adjective** derived from the noun in brackets in each space. One has already been done for you.

If you are looking for an __interesting__ [interest] hobby, you could

learn a _____ [music] instrument. It can be very rewarding

and will bring you _____ [end] enjoyment.

1 mark

23 Read the sentences below. Tick the **two** sentences which are **formal**.

Tick **two** boxes.

She is coming for dinner, isn't she? ☐

The owner insisted that we remove our shoes. ☐

If I was taller, I'd be able to reach the top shelf. ☐

They had a superb painting on the wall. ☐

1 mark

Key Stage Two English

Set A
Grammar, Punctuation and Spelling

Paper 2: Spelling

First name	
Middle name	
Last name	
School	

Date of birth	Day		Month		Year	

Total marks

Spelling Test

1. She tried to help him by _____ the door.

2. Squirrels are _____ found in forests.

3. There wasn't a single _____ left on the plate.

4. Angela had another _____ of pizza.

5. She was _____ from a cold all week.

6. They all agreed that he had been very _____ .

7. The building's _____ took a long time.

8. The weather had been _____ all summer.

9. He resisted the _____ to open the present.

10. The doctor wrote an _____ note for her.

11. It was the _____ time we had visited them.

12. He is a _____ person — he does not take risks.

13. There was some _____ about where we

were meeting.

14. It took a lot of _____ to perform at the concert.

15. My uncle applied for the job _____ at the factory.

16. He took the car to a professional _____ .

17. Their balcony gave them a _____ view of the sea.

18. Mum's favourite vase was a _____ shape.

19. They had a _____ meeting with the head teacher.

20. Alex had a successful career as a _____ .

END OF TEST

[Blank Page]

24 Read the sentences below. Change all the underlined verbs from the **present** tense to the **simple past** tense.

One has already been done for you.

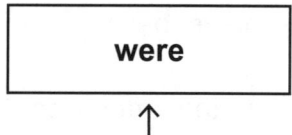

The three children <u>are</u> late for school.

My sister and I <u>sleep</u> for eight hours every night.

The dogs <u>enjoy</u> playing with tennis balls.

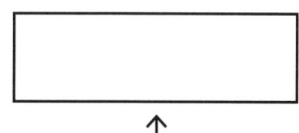

Alexander <u>swims</u> for the school's team.

1 mark

25 Read the sentence below.
Circle the **possessive pronoun**.

She said that the log cabin is ours for the whole weekend.

1 mark

26 Read the sentences below.
Circle the words which need capital letters.

my brother's best friend is called james williams. he is having a birthday

party in manchester next saturday at two o'clock in the afternoon.

1 mark

27 Read the sentences below.
Tick the sentence which is written in the **passive voice**.

Tick **one** box.

The animal shelter put an advert in the local paper. ☐

The charity buffet was arranged for Tuesday. ☐

The book club planned where to meet. ☐

The company posted leaflets to all the houses. ☐

1 mark

28 Read the sentences below.
Circle all the **conjunctions**.

Before we go to the airport, we should check the flight times again.

We need to hurry and get a taxi if we want to get there on time.

29 a) Add a **comma** in the sentence below so that it is clear that **only** Lindsay and Jasmine went home.

After they paid Ryan Lindsay and Jasmine went home.

b) Add **commas** in the sentence below so that it is clear that **all** three children went home.

After they paid Ryan Lindsay and Jasmine went home.

30 Read the sentence below.
Insert the missing **dashes** so that the sentence is punctuated correctly.

My cousins Rachael and Phillip will pick me up so we can go to the play.

1 mark

31 Read the sentences below.
Draw a line to show which words the **pronoun** 'They' replaces.

Anna and Diego baked lots of cakes on Sunday. **They** had a lot of washing up
to do but their families and their friends at school enjoyed eating the cakes.

Pronoun   **Noun**

the cakes

the friends

They

Anna and Diego

the families

1 mark

32 Read the sentence below.
Rewrite the sentence as **direct speech**. Make sure you use correct punctuation.

He asked if she enjoyed the film.

He asked her, _____

_____

1 mark

33 Explain how the different **prefixes** in the two sentences below change their meanings.

Katie <u>refilled</u> the bucket.

This means that the bucket _____

_____

Katie <u>overfilled</u> the bucket.

This means that the bucket _____

_____

1 mark

34 Read the sentences below.
Tick the sentence which uses a **dash** correctly.

Tick **one** box.

Rebecca went into the dining — room it was extremely quiet. ☐

Rebecca went into the dining room — it was extremely quiet. ☐

Rebecca went into the dining room it was — extremely quiet. ☐

Rebecca went into the dining room it — was extremely quiet. ☐

1 mark

35 Read the sentences below.
Tick the sentence which uses **hyphens** correctly.

Tick **one** box.

We are getting a twelve-week old kitten tomorrow. ☐

We are getting a twelve-week-old kitten tomorrow. ☐

We are getting a twelve-week-old-kitten tomorrow. ☐

We are getting a twelve week-old kitten tomorrow. ☐

1 mark

36 Read the sentence below.
Circle the **relative pronoun** in the sentence.

After lunch, we went back on the roller coaster rides that we had

already been on.

37 Read the sentence below.
Insert the missing **commas** so that the sentence is punctuated correctly.

Amy who lives near the coast loves sailing.

38 Rewrite the sentence below by adding a **subordinate clause** to it.
Make sure you use correct punctuation.

Samantha went to the supermarket.

_____

_____

1 mark

39 Read the sentence below.
Underline the longest **noun phrase** there is in the sentence.

My friend and her family live in the old house next to the park.

1 mark

40 Put a tick in each row of the table below to show whether the conjunction in bold is a **co-ordinating conjunction** or **subordinating conjunction**.

Sentence	Co-ordinating conjunction	Subordinating conjunction
Until we get a television, we won't be able to watch the matches.		
We are running out of kitchen roll, **so** we need to go to the shop.		
Anthony hates smoothies, **yet** he loves fruit juice.		

1 mark

41 Read the sentence below and circle all the **determiners**.

We went to three shops in the town centre,

but we couldn't find any peppers.

1 mark

42 Read the sentence below.
What is 'a world-famous breakdancing group' an example of?

A world-famous breakdancing group is performing at the stadium tonight.

Tick **one** box.

a main clause ☐

an adverbial phrase ☐

a subordinate clause ☐

a noun phrase ☐

1 mark

43 Complete the sentence below by filling in the gaps with the **present progressive** form of the verbs in the boxes.

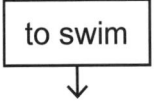

to play

The girls _____ a game of volleyball on the beach,

to swim

and their brother _____ in the sea.

1 mark

44 Put a letter in each box to show which **word class** the words belong to.

determiner	adjective	preposition	adverb
A	B	C	D

A new boy started at my school today. He was very friendly.

 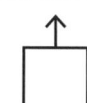 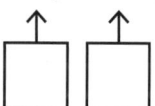

1 mark

45 Look at the **word family** below.
What does the root '**loc**' mean in this word family?

locate   relocation   local

Tick **one** box.

build   ☐

improve   ☐

friendly   ☐

place   ☐

1 mark

46 Read the two sentences below. Explain how the meaning of the sentence is changed when the **commas** are added.

Cats which are often active at night make the best pets.

Cats, which are often active at night, make the best pets.

_____

_____

1 mark

47 Read the information in the box below. Write one sentence that lists all this information. Make sure you use correct punctuation.

Shopping list
birthday card (for Dad)
a loaf of bread
a pint of milk
self-raising flour

_____

_____

1 mark

48 The sentence below is missing a **punctuation mark** in the place the arrow is pointing at. Which punctuation mark should be used?

Ruth whispered quietly, "We're not really supposed to talk about it"
Emily couldn't believe what she was hearing. ↑

Tick **one** box.

comma ☐

full stop ☐

exclamation mark ☐

semi-colon ☐

1 mark

49 Read the sentences below.
Tick the sentence which uses the **subjunctive form**.

Tick **one** box.

Their parents told them that they are careful. ☐

Their parents asked them to be careful. ☐

Their parents asked that they be careful. ☐

Their parents requested that they are careful. ☐

1 mark

END OF TEST

[Blank Page]

Key Stage Two English

Set B
Grammar, Punctuation and Spelling

Paper 1: Questions
45 minutes

First name	
Middle name	
Last name	
School	

Date of birth	Day		Month		Year	

Paper 2, the spelling task, is a pull-out section in the middle of the booklet.

Total marks

[Blank Page]

Instructions

This booklet tests your **grammar**, **vocabulary** and **punctuation**. The test has different question types, which you will need to answer in different ways. Each question has a space for you to give your answer. This will show you the type of answer to give:

Multiple-choice answers: you can answer these questions without writing any words. You might have to tick a box, circle a word or draw lines between different words. Read the instructions for each question carefully, as they will tell you what to do.

Short answers: these questions have a line or a box for your answer. This shows that you need to write something. It could be a word, a short phrase or a sentence.

There is a mark box next to each question. It tells you the maximum number of marks for that question.

Do not start until your teacher tells you to. Once you have started the test, work through the booklet until you are told to stop.

You will have 45 minutes to answer all the questions.

1 Read the sentence below.
Which **word class** does the word '**early**' belong to?

We had an **early** dinner because we were very hungry.

Tick **one** box.

noun ☐

verb ☐

adjective ☐

adverb ☐

2 Read the sentence below.
Tick the **pair of verbs** which completes the sentence correctly.

We _____ going to go on holiday in July, but now we

_____ going in August.

Tick **one** box.

are   are   ☐

were   were   ☐

are   were   ☐

were   are   ☐

3 Tick the most appropriate punctuation mark to end this sentence.

We're inviting people to my birthday party, aren't we

Tick **one** box.

. ☐

? ☐

! ☐

... ☐

1 mark

4 The sentence below is missing an **exclamation mark**.
Tick **one** box to show where the exclamation mark should go.

"How fantastic that is" cried Alex, running over to hug Shahnaz.

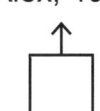 ☐   ☐   ☐   ☐

1 mark

5 Read the options below.
Tick the option that uses **full stops** correctly.

Tick **one** box.

I got a new bike today it's red and white. With a
basket. On the front so I can carry things.

☐

I got a new bike. Today it's red and white with a
basket on the front. So I can carry things.

☐

I got a new bike today. It's red and white with a
basket on the front so I can carry things.

☐

I got a new bike today it's red and white with a
basket on the front so I can carry things.

☐

1 mark

6 Read the sentences below.
Choose a **conjunction** from the box to fill each gap and write it on the line.
You can only use each conjunction **once**.

that	while	before

My brother and I needed to clean our bedrooms _____ going to

the party. I did the vacuuming _____ my brother made the beds.

We were pleased _____ we finished in time.

1 mark

7 Read the sentences below.
Tick the sentence which is in the **present progressive tense**.

Tick **one** box.

He seemed very quiet yesterday. ☐

She is tidying her bedroom. ☐

We waited for fifteen minutes. ☐

They travelled from Paris to London. ☐

1 mark

8 Look at the table below. Put a tick in each row to show whether each sentence is a **statement** or a **command**.

Sentence	Statement	Command
I asked if I could open my present.		
Don't spend too much money on the present.		
She might buy me a present.		

1 mark

9 Read the sentence below. Insert the missing **comma** so that the sentence is punctuated correctly.

Susan said " We need to leave as early as possible . "

1 mark

10 Read the sentence below.
Tick the pair of **pronouns** that best completes the sentence.

The raincoat is _____ but the walking boots are _____.

Tick **one** box.

her	he	☐
hers	his	☐
her	his	☐
hers	he	☐

1 mark

11 Circle all the words in the sentence below that should have an **apostrophe**.

Were travelling in Dads car to visit my two sisters.

I cant wait to see them.

1 mark

12 Read the sentence below.
Insert the missing **comma** so that the sentence is punctuated correctly.

Smiling widely Jenny handed Chris the fluffy puppy.

1 mark

13 Read the sentences below.
Circle the correct word in brackets to complete each sentence.

He walked **(slowly / slow)** along the beach.

Please will you pass me **(them / those)** potatoes?

She **(ain't / isn't)** having a very good time on her holiday.

1 mark

14 Read the sentence below. Replace the underlined word with a **more formal** word. Write the word in the box.

He <u>chucked</u> the apple into the bin.

1 mark

15 Read the sentence below.
Insert **three commas** so that the sentence is punctuated correctly.

Rachel Frances and Rosie who lives next door came to the party.

1 mark

16 Draw lines to match each word to the correct **prefix** to change its meaning.

Prefix	Word
im	able
un	react
over	possible

1 mark

17 Read the sentence below.
Circle the two words that show the **tense** in the sentence.

It was a really nice day yesterday, so we walked to the park.

1 mark

18 What is the **name** of the punctuation mark immediately after the word <u>long</u> in the sentence below?

They didn't have a long-term plan for where they were going to live.

_____

1 mark

19 Put a tick in each row of the table to show whether each sentence is in the **present progressive** or the **past progressive**.

Sentence	Present progressive	Past progressive
Jack was baking a cake for two hours.		
Jack is planning to open his own bakery.		
Jack's cakes are baking in the oven right now.		

1 mark

20 Read the sentences below.
Circle all of the **conjunctions**.

We haven't been on holiday since my baby brother was born.

Would you like orange juice or milk?

I wanted to buy her a present because it was her birthday.

1 mark

21 Read the sentences below.
Tick **all** the sentences that contain a **preposition**.

I have a clarinet lesson after school. ☐

We had ice cream before we left. ☐

My scooter is in the garden shed. ☐

They had some decorations above the door. ☐

1 mark

22 Read the sentences below.
Tick the **two** sentences which contain a **modal verb**.

Tick **two** boxes.

She always brings nice sandwiches to school. ☐

He said he was finishing his homework. ☐

Sophie will sit next to me on the bus. ☐

They could complete the journey in two hours. ☐

1 mark

Key Stage Two English

Set B
Grammar, Punctuation and Spelling

Paper 2: Spelling

First name	
Middle name	
Last name	
School	

Date of birth	Day		Month		Year	

Total marks

Spelling Test

1. He was careful not to _____ his socks.

2. The dog wanted to _____ its bone.

3. The _____ woman shook the man's hand.

4. Abdullah had _____ to buy a ticket.

5. They had a _____ morning by the pool.

6. She bought some plasters from the _____ .

7. Sophie felt very _____ of Mo's new bike.

8. The assistant showed them a _____ of colours.

9. They had to walk _____ deep water to get back to the car.

10. His description of the location was _____ .

11. They needed some _____ to bake the bread.

12. The _____ from the mountain was tiring.

13. She made some _____ comments.

14. He gave them _____ to look around his house.

15. He acted _____ during the argument.

16. The girl _____ several gifts for her birthday.

17. We visited the lion _____ at the zoo.

18. The army was planning an _____ .

19. The children made a _____ amount of noise.

20. He didn't mean to be _____ .

END OF TEST

[Blank Page]

23 Read the sentence below. Put **V** in the box under the **verb**, **S** in the box under the **subject** and **O** in the box under the **object**.

Riyad knits cardigans.

↑ ↑ ↑
☐ ☐ ☐

1 mark

24 Write your own sentence using the word '**turn**' as a **verb**.
Use correct punctuation in your sentence. Do not change the word '**turn**'.

_____

1 mark

Write your own sentence using the word '**turn**' as a **noun**.
Use correct punctuation in your sentence. Do not change the word '**turn**'.

_____

1 mark

25 The sentence below contains **one** error.
Circle the error and write the correction in the box.

The actors was rehearsing their lines backstage.

[ ]

1 mark

26 Look at the table below. Change the statement into a **question**.
Write the question in the right-hand column.

Statement	Question
She plays the piano.	

1 mark

27 Read the sentences below. Insert the missing **inverted commas** so that the sentences are punctuated correctly.

"Wait a minute, Dad called. Don't forget to take your jacket.

28 The sentence below is missing a **dash**.
Tick **one** box to show where the dash should go.

We couldn't get her the new necklace it was too expensive.

 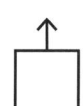 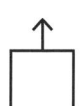 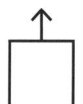

29 Put a tick in each row of the table below to show whether the words in bold are **adjectives** or **adverbs**.

Sentence	Adjective	Adverb
He put the vase down **carefully**.		
We sat in the **chilly** living room.		
Her new curtains are **lovely**.		
They arrived **late** for the flight.		

1 mark

30 Rewrite the sentence below so it starts with the **adverbial**. Only use the words from the sentence, and make sure you use correct punctuation.

We are going to a barbecue this evening.

_____

_____

1 mark

31 a) Give an explanation of the word **antonym**.

_____

_____

1 mark

b) Give one word that is an **antonym** of <u>thorough</u>.

_____

1 mark

32 Read the sentences below.
Tick the sentence which uses a **colon** correctly.

Tick **one** box.

Ben was tired he hadn't slept: very well. ☐

Ben was tired: he hadn't slept very well. ☐

Ben was: tired he hadn't slept very well. ☐

Ben was tired he hadn't: slept very well. ☐

1 mark

33 Read the passage below. Underline the verb form that is in the **past perfect**.

My mum's friend Ian came to our house for dinner last night.

He <u>had been</u> on holiday for two weeks so he was telling us all about it.

1 mark

34 Read the sentence below and circle the **relative pronoun**.

The girl (who) lives next door goes to judo classes.

1 mark

35 Read the sentences below and circle all the **determiners**.

We decided to make some cookies for the baking competition. We made

four batches before we were happy with them.

36 Read the sentence below and underline the **relative clause**.

Lisa was fond of the quilt that she had owned since birth.

37 Put a different **suffix** at the end of each word below to make it an **adjective**.

delight _____

worth _____

option _____

1 mark

38 Look at the table below. Add your own words before and after the noun to make your own **noun phrase**.

One has already been done for you.

Noun	Noun phrase
the curtains	the old curtains in the dining room
the skateboard	

1 mark

39 Read the sentences below and circle the two **adverbs**.

Samantha spoke confidently during class presentations. She also

impressed everyone with her written work.

1 mark

40 Put a tick in each row of the table to show whether the words in **bold** are a **noun phrase** or a **subordinate clause**.

Sentence	Noun phrase	Subordinate clause
My brother's best friend has a holiday home in Spain.		
Even if we get the last bus, we will still be on time for the play.		
We can't watch the film **until we fix the DVD player**.		

1 mark

41 Read the sentence below. Explain why a **pair of brackets** has been used in this sentence.

Fay (my oldest sister) is going to Australia for four weeks in December.

_____

_____

1 mark

42 Look at the **word family** below.
What does the root '**nov**' mean in this word family?

renovate   novelty   innovate

Tick **one** box.

repair   ☐

new   ☐

invent   ☐

now   ☐

1 mark

43 Rewrite the sentence below so it is in the **active voice**.
Use the words from the sentence and remove any words where appropriate.
Make sure you use correct punctuation.

My car was repaired by the garage.

_____

_____

1 mark

44 Complete the sentence below by ticking the option that correctly introduces the **subordinate clause**.

We decided to get the train to the airport _____ drive and risk being late because of the traffic.

Tick **one** box.

although ☐

even though ☐

since ☐

rather than ☐

1 mark

45 Complete the sentence below by filling in the gap with a **possessive pronoun**.

The train set is _____.

1 mark

46 The word 'after' can be either a **subordinating conjunction** or a **preposition**. Put a tick in each row to show which form '**after**' takes in each sentence.

Sentence	Preposition	Subordinating conjunction
After we'd been to the concert, we had dinner at a restaurant.		
I won't go there again **after** such a terrible experience.		
We will give the tent back to him **after** we return from the trip.		

1 mark

47 Tick the option below that completes the sentence in the **subjunctive form**.

If I _____ you, I would buy it as soon as possible.

Tick **one** box.

had been ☐

am ☐

were ☐

was ☐

48 Read the sentences below.
Tick the sentence which uses **commas** correctly.

Tick **one** box.

Next week, my cousin, who loves travelling, is going to Paris. ☐

Next week my cousin who loves travelling, is going to Paris. ☐

Next week my cousin, who loves travelling, is going to Paris. ☐

Next week, my cousin, who loves travelling is going to Paris. ☐

END OF TEST

[Blank Page]

KS2 English / Set B / GP&S Paper 1

EHP27U

CGP

Key Stage Two

English

SATS Practice Papers

Instructions with Answers & Mark Scheme

Contents

Published by CGP

Editors:
Joe Brazier, Joanna Daniels, Catherine Heygate,
Cathy Lear, Holly Robinson, Matt Topping.

With thanks to Emma Crighton, Alison Griffin
and Rebecca Tate for the proofreading.
Also thanks to Jan Greenway for the copyright research.

Acknowledgements for Answer Booklet:
National Curriculum references on page 4, 8, 12, 16, 20 and 21 reproduced under the terms of the Open
Government Licence v3.0. http://www.nationalarchives.gov.uk/doc/open-government-licence/version/3/

Acknowledgements for Reading Set A:
With thanks to iStock.com for permission to use the images on pages 1, 2 and 3.
With thanks to Andy Lear for permission to use the image on page 6.

Acknowledgements for Reading Set B:
With thanks to iStock.com for permission to use the images on pages 1, 2 and 3.

Clipart from Corel®
Printed by Elanders Ltd, Newcastle upon Tyne.

Text, design and original illustrations
© Coordination Group Publications Ltd. (CGP) 2020
All rights reserved.

Test Contents

There are **two sets** of practice papers in this pack.
Each set has:

Reading Test   **50 marks**
1 hour
(reading booklet, and question and answer booklet)

Grammar, Punctuation and Spelling Paper 1 — Questions   **50 marks**
45 minutes
(question and answer booklet)

Grammar, Punctuation and Spelling Paper 2 — Spelling Task   **20 marks**
About 15 minutes
(pull-out question and answer booklet found in the middle of Grammar, Punctuation and Spelling Paper 1)

The Spelling Task needs to be read out to the child sitting the test.
The Spelling Task Scripts can be found on pages 22 and 23 of this booklet.

Marking the Tests

The scores for these practice papers will give you a pretty good idea of whether a pupil is on track to achieve the **expected standard** in **Reading** and in **Grammar, Punctuation and Spelling**.

Reading

There's a total of **50** marks available.

The mark needed to achieve the **expected standard** varies from year to year, but if they get a total of **21** or more then they should be on track.

Grammar, Punctuation and Spelling

	Marks available
Paper 1: Short Answer Questions	50
Paper 2: Spelling Task	20
Total:	**70**

Add up the marks in the two papers to give a score out of **70**. Again, the mark needed to achieve the **expected standard** varies from year to year, but if they get a total of **44** or more then they should be on track. (The writing element of the national curriculum is assessed by the class teacher.)

Set A: Reading

Content Domain Coverage

(Shows the aspects of reading assessed in the Set A reading paper)

	2a	2b	2c	2d	2e	2f	2g	2h
	Give / explain the meaning of words in context.	*Retrieve and record information / identify key details from fiction and non-fiction.*	*Summarise main ideas from more than one paragraph.*	*Make inferences from the text / explain and justify inferences with evidence from the text.*	*Predict what might happen from details stated and implied.*	*Identify / explain how information / narrative content is related and contributes to meaning as a whole.*	*Identify / explain how meaning is enhanced through choice of words and phrases.*	*Make comparisons within the text.*
Qu.			Section 1 – The Fisherman					
1		1						
2	1							
3				1				
4		1						
5	1							
6	1							
7		2						
8				1				
9				2				
Qu.			Section 2 – Summit Success for Intrepid Becky					
10		1						
11	1							
12		1						
13		1						
14		1						
15	1							
16		1						
17				1				
18		1						
19							2	
20				1				
21				1				
22	2							
23				2				
24				2				
Qu.			Section 3 – Wild Camping					
25a		1						
25b	1							
25c		1						
25d		1						
26				1				
27				1				
28	1							
29		1						
30		1						
31							1	
32			1					
33	1							
34				1				
35a						1		
35b								1
36				2				
37				3				

Set A: Reading – Answers

Section 1 — The Fisherman

Qu.	Answer	Marking notes	Marks *(Domain)*
1	Refers to dawn / early in the morning.		**1** *(2b)*
2	in bed		**1** *(2a)*
3	Refers to it being the food he eats. Refers to it being fish that he sells to make money.	1 mark for reference to either of the acceptable answers.	**1** *(2d)*
4	Recognition that he spends half of his life on the shore / on land and half of it at sea.		**1** *(2b)*
5	odd		**1** *(2a)*
6	wondrous		**1** *(2a)*
7	boats sky tides things of wonder winds things of fear clouds wondrous tales	1 mark for 2 or 3 correct. 2 marks for 4 correct.	**2** *(2b)*
8	Refers to him not being interested in city things. Refers to him disliking city things. Refers to him not being familiar with city things.	1 mark for reference to any of the acceptable answers.	**1** *(2d)*
9	Acceptable points and possible evidence: • Hardworking, e.g. he gets up early to fish when everyone else is 'abed'. • Strange / mysterious, e.g. he has 'curious eyes' that make you feel 'queer'. • Interesting, e.g. he tells 'wondrous tales'. • Unfriendly / grumpy, e.g. he doesn't want to know about 'city things'. • Knowledgeable / wise, e.g. 'He knows so much'. • Experienced / well-travelled, e.g. he has seen 'many things'. • Isolated / different, e.g. he is 'not quite / The same' as other people. **Do not accept** any reference to the fisherman being curious / inquisitive.	1 mark for 1 acceptable point. 2 marks for 2 acceptable points, or 1 acceptable point supported with evidence.	**2** *(2d)*

Section 2 — Summit Success for Intrepid Becky

Qu.	Answer	Marking notes	Marks (Domain)
10	librarian		**1** (2b)
11	ferocious		**1** (2a)
12	Mont Blanc is the highest mountain in Western Europe. — True Mont Blanc is on the border between France and Switzerland. — False Mont Blanc's summit is permanently covered in snow. — True Becky is 33 years old. — False	1 mark for all 4 correct.	**1** (2b)
13	Recognition that Becky had never climbed higher than 1000m. Recognition that Becky had never been on a mountain in the snow.	1 mark for both correct.	**1** (2b)
14	Recognition that they are spikes that fit to the bottom of your shoes.		**1** (2b)
15	Refers to changing a safe situation into a dangerous / bad one.		**1** (2a)
16	difficulty breathing feeling sick feeling dizzy	1 mark for 2 correct answers.	**1** (2b)
17	Refers to her feet feeling like they were stuck in cement. **Do not accept** any reference to her lungs burning / her doubts about whether she could reach the top.		**1** (2d)
18	Refers to Jean-Claude encouraging her. Refers to her thinking of / remembering the children at the hospital.	1 mark for reference to either of the acceptable answers.	**1** (2b)
19	tricky demanding tough technical dangerous tackled gruelling problem epic challenge difficult struggle hardest	1 mark for 1 or 2 words correct. 2 marks for 3 words correct.	**2** (2g)
20	Refers to the writer describing Becky's climb as an 'epic achievement'.		**1** (2d)
21	Becky raised an astonishing amount of money. — Opinion Becky did some training before climbing Mont Blanc. — Fact Holden Park is a children's hospital. — Fact Kamal received brilliant care at the hospital. — Opinion	1 mark for all 4 correct.	**1** (2d)
22	challenging ——— impact willingness ——— elated impression ——— demanding thrilled ——— readiness	1 mark for 2 or 3 correct. 2 marks for all 4 correct.	**2** (2a)
23	Acceptable points: • Becky's willingness to climb the mountain for charity 'made a real impression' on her. • She donated to Becky's cause. • She was 'thrilled' when she heard that Becky's climb had been successful. • She thinks it's 'wonderful' that Becky raised so much money.	1 mark for 1 acceptable point. 2 marks for 2 acceptable points.	**2** (2d)
24	Acceptable points: • It shows that raising money can help the children at Holden Park. • It shows that people respond positively when someone is trying to raise money. • It suggests ways in which the reader can raise money / invites them to fundraising events. • It tells the reader that Holden Park needs more money.	1 mark for 1 acceptable point. 2 marks for 2 acceptable points.	**2** (2d)

Section 3 — Wild Camping

Qu.	Answer	Marking notes	Marks (Domain)
25a	in the woods.		1 (2b)
25b	excitedly.		1 (2a)
25c	a hamster.		1 (2b)
25d	lighting the fire.		1 (2b)
26	Refers to Callum not liking the way his dad describes the trip. Refers to Callum thinking it's 'bad' that they're going to stay in the woods. Refers to Callum being 'slumped' in the car seat.	1 mark for reference to any of the acceptable answers.	1 (2d)
27	Refers to his family being excited by the hamster. Refers to his family cuddling / cooing over the hamster.	1 mark for reference to either of the acceptable answers.	1 (2d)
28	frantic		1 (2a)
29	It scuttled up his arm. It jumped into his lap. It ran across his chest. It bit him on the finger.	1 mark for any 2 correct answers.	1 (2b)
30	rustling leaves cooing pigeons crunching twigs towering trees	1 mark for any 2 correct answers.	1 (2b)
31	Refers to the birds, bugs and beasts being: frightening threatening numerous violent dangerous organised	1 mark for reference to any of the acceptable answers.	1 (2g)
32	Callum sees and hears things that scare him.		1 (2c)
33	Bewildered		1 (2a)
34	Refers to Callum's dad not believing Callum. Refers to Callum's dad thinking Callum is overreacting / being silly / joking.	1 mark for reference to any of the acceptable answers.	1 (2d)
35a	"Get out! Hey! Ouch!" **Also accept:** "Get out!"		1 (2f)
35b	Refers to him being cheery / upbeat / enthusiastic before and now him being scared / startled / angry.		1 (2h)
36	Acceptable points and possible evidence: • Anxious, e.g. Callum was 'terrified' of a rabbit. • Caring, e.g. Callum 'gently ushered the rabbit out' of the tent. • Brave, e.g. Callum 'grabbed the rabbit' despite being 'terrified' of it. • Calm, e.g. Callum released the rabbit 'without saying anything'. • Rational / sensible, e.g. he realised the 'terrible creature' was just a rabbit before his dad did.	1 mark for 1 acceptable point. 2 marks for 2 acceptable points, or 1 acceptable point supported with evidence.	2 (2d)
37	Acceptable points (yes / maybe): • Callum had a scary experience with a rabbit that made him 'terrified'. • Callum didn't say anything when he released the rabbit, suggesting it still terrified him. • The 'forest's hidden army' had made Callum nervous throughout the trip. • Callum had always been scared of 'pretty much anything that moved'. • Callum grabbed the rabbit 'without thinking' so he might not have realised that he was scared of it. Acceptable points (no / maybe): • Callum had 'vowed' never to hold an animal again, but held the rabbit. • Callum was 'relieved' it was only a rabbit, suggesting he wasn't scared of it. • Callum 'gently' released the rabbit, suggesting he cared about it. • He grabbed the rabbit without hesitating, suggesting he was over his fear. • The rabbit didn't hurt him, so he may have learnt animals can be harmless.	1 mark for 1 acceptable point. 2 marks for 2 acceptable points. 3 marks for 3 acceptable points.	3 (2e)

Set B: Reading

Content Domain Coverage

(Shows the aspects of reading assessed in the Set B reading paper)

	2a	2b	2c	2d	2e	2f	2g	2h
	Give / explain the meaning of words in context.	*Retrieve and record information / identify key details from fiction and non-fiction.*	*Summarise main ideas from more than one paragraph.*	*Make inferences from the text / explain and justify inferences with evidence from the text.*	*Predict what might happen from details stated and implied.*	*Identify / explain how information / narrative content is related and contributes to meaning as a whole.*	*Identify / explain how meaning is enhanced through choice of words and phrases.*	*Make comparisons within the text.*
Qu.				Section 1 – The Secret of the Cave				
1a	1							
1b		1						
1c		1						
2	1							
3		2						
4		1						
5							1	
6				2				
7		1						
8				2				
9		1						
10				1				
11		1						
12				1				
Qu.				Section 2 – Hedgehogs				
13		1						
14	1							
15		1						
16				2				
17							1	
18		2						
19				1				
20		1						
21		1						
22				2				
23	1							
24		1						
25				1				
Qu.				Section 3 – The War of the Worlds				
26	1							
27		1						
28	1							
29		1						
30		1						
31		1						
32				1				
33	2							
34				1				
35							1	
36				3				
37			1					
38					2			

© CGP 2020

Set B: Reading – Answers

Section 1 — The Secret of the Cave

Qu.	Answer	Marking notes	Marks (Domain)
1a	quickly.		1 (2a)
1b	coins.		1 (2b)
1c	going to get their dinghy.		1 (2b)
2	swarms		1 (2a)
3	a green turtle colourful fish a coral reef	1 mark for 1 or 2 correct. 2 marks for 3 correct.	2 (2b)
4	Refers to Ben tapping / touching Jack on the shoulder.		1 (2b)
5	Refers to the cave looking scary / threatening. Refers to the cave being jagged / rocky. Refers to the cave being large. Refers to the cave looking dangerous. Refers to the cave being dark.	1 mark for reference to any of the acceptable answers.	1 (2g)
6	Refers to Jack saying it might be dangerous. Refers to Jack being nervous. Refers to Jack eyeing the jagged rocks / thrashing waves. Refers to Jack hesitating.	1 mark for reference to 1 of the acceptable answers. 2 marks for reference to 2 of the acceptable answers.	2 (2d)
7	Refers to Ben setting off before Jack. Refers to Ben being a stronger swimmer than Jack. Refers to Jack's panic making it harder for him to swim.	1 mark for reference to any of the acceptable answers.	1 (2b)
8	Refers to Ben not saying anything. Refers to Ben's eyes being wide. Refers to the boys laughing in disbelief.	1 mark for reference to 1 of the acceptable answers. 2 marks for reference to 2 of the acceptable answers.	2 (2d)
9	Refers to the crate having been washed into the cave by the sea. **Do not accept** answers that only refer to the crate being lost at sea.		1 (2b)
10	Refers to the coins being very valuable. Refers to the crate's owner being grateful to the boys for returning it.	1 mark for reference to either of the acceptable answers.	1 (2d)
11	The sea is rough inside the cave. — False Ben suggests carrying the crate to the beach in a dinghy. — True The crate is on a rocky ledge. — True Jack wants to swim back to the beach with the crate. — False	1 mark for all 4 correct.	1 (2b)
12	Refers to the men scowling at the boys.		1 (2d)

Section 2 — Hedgehogs

Qu.	Answer	Marking notes	Marks (Domain)
13	They forage around in hedges. They make grunting, pig-like noises.	1 mark for both correct.	**1** (2b)
14	identifiable		**1** (2a)
15	Refers to hedgehogs curling up into a ball.		**1** (2b)
16	Refers to there being fewer creatures for hedgehogs to eat. Refers to hedgehogs hibernating. Refers to hedgehogs' metabolism slowing down. Refers to hedgehogs getting their energy from surplus fat / gorging in the summer.	1 mark for reference to 1 of the acceptable answers. 2 marks for reference to 2 of the acceptable answers.	**2** (2d)
17	Refers to hedgehogs being keen / happy to eat. Refers to hedgehogs eating a lot / too much / greedily.	1 mark for reference to either of the acceptable answers.	**1** (2g)
18	Refers to them hibernating between November and March. Refers to them being nocturnal / sleeping during the day.	1 mark for reference to 1 of the acceptable answers. 2 marks for reference to 2 of the acceptable answers.	**2** (2b)
19	Refers to the hedgehog eating garden pests.		**1** (2d)
20	Refers to hedgehogs being wild animals. Refers to hedgehogs needing to roam (over a wide area). Refers to hedgehogs not being able to get enough food if they are confined to just one garden.	1 mark for reference to any of the acceptable answers.	**1** (2b)
21	There is only one species of hedgehog in the world. — False There is less food available for hedgehogs in winter. — True You should give cows' milk to hedgehogs. — False Hedgehogs can get through hedges. — True	1 mark for all 4 correct.	**1** (2b)
22	Acceptable points (yes / maybe): • Putting out food could 'supplement their diet'. • Sightings of hedgehogs are rare, so putting food out would give more people the chance to see them. • Putting out food out for hedgehogs could help gardeners, as hedgehogs eat pests that could damage their plants. Acceptable points (no / maybe): • Hedgehogs are 'perfectly capable of finding their own food.' • Some foods such as 'cows' milk' can be harmful or even fatal to hedgehogs. • The food could be eaten by 'larger animals' before hedgehogs can get to it.	1 mark for 1 acceptable point. 2 marks for 2 acceptable points.	**2** (2d)
23	Refers to behaving in the same way as you.		**1** (2a)
24	Refers to hedgehogs using them to build a nest. Refers to hedgehogs hibernating in them. Refers to hedgehogs sleeping in them.	1 mark for reference to 2 of the acceptable answers.	**1** (2b)
25	Refers to the lawn mower harming / killing the hedgehogs.		**1** (2d)

Section 3 — The War of the Worlds

Qu.	Answer	Marking notes	Marks (Domain)
26	Refers to it moving very fast. Refers to it being in a hurry to land on Earth.	1 mark for reference to either of the acceptable answers.	1 (2a)
27	eastward / to the east		1 (2b)
28	authority		1 (2a)
29	Refers to his window facing towards where it was falling / the blinds being up. Refers to him enjoying / loving looking up at the night sky. Refers to him being by the window when it was falling. Refers to the meteorite making a hissing sound as it travelled. Refers to many other people having seen the meteorite.	1 mark for reference to 2 of the acceptable answers.	1 (2b)
30	between Horsell, Ottershaw and Woking		1 (2b)
31	It created an enormous hole.　It set the heather on fire. It threw sand and gravel everywhere.　It made / gave off smoke. It formed heaps of sand and gravel.	1 mark for reference to 2 of the acceptable answers.	1 (2b)
32	Refers to the Thing being almost entirely buried in sand. Refers to the Thing having splintered a tree on its descent. **Do not accept** answers that refer to the Thing being hot.	1 mark for reference to either of the acceptable answers.	1 (2d)
33	buried — exposed amidst — prevent uncovered — among forbid — embedded (buried→embedded, amidst→among, uncovered→exposed, forbid→prevent)	1 mark for 2 or 3 correct. 2 marks for all 4 correct.	2 (2a)
34	Refers to the Thing having an unusual shape. Refers to it being an unusual colour. Refers to it having a strange appearance. Refers to its arrival having been planned / it being deliberately sent to Earth. **Do not accept** reference to it looking like it was designed / man-made.	1 mark for reference to any of the acceptable answers.	1 (2d)
35	Then the thing came upon him in a flash. Something within the cylinder was unscrewing the top!	1 mark for either of the acceptable answers.	1 (2f)
36	Acceptable points and possible evidence: • Surprised, e.g. Ogilvy was surprised at its 'size and more so at the shape'. • Puzzled, e.g. most meteorites are 'rounded' but the Thing wasn't round. • Scared, e.g. the noise of a piece falling off 'brought his heart into his mouth'. • Curious, e.g. he climbed into the pit so he could see the Thing 'more clearly.' • Worried, e.g. he would have been worried when he realised that something inside the cylinder was 'unscrewing the top'. • Amazed, e.g. he stared at its 'strange appearance'. • Confused, e.g. he 'scarcely understood' what was happening when the top of the meteorite began to unscrew.	1 mark for 1 acceptable point. 2 marks for 2 acceptable points, or 1 acceptable point supported with evidence. 3 marks for 3 acceptable points, or 2 acceptable points with at least one supported with evidence.	3 (2d)
37	Ogilvy climbs down into the pit. — 5 A meteorite falls to Earth. — 1 A description of the meteorite's appearance. — 3 The meteorite is found. — 2 Ogilvy realises the truth. — 6 Ash is falling off the meteorite. — 4	1 mark for all 5 correct.	1 (2c)
38	Possible predictions and evidence: • Something will come out of the cylinder, e.g. there was something 'within' it. • An alien will appear, e.g. Ogilvy thinks the cylinder has been sent to Earth deliberately. • More cylinders will land, e.g. this was the 'first' shooting star. **Do not accept** answers that speculate about what will happen next without reference to what has already happened in the text.	1 mark for 1 acceptable point. 2 marks for 2 acceptable points, or 1 acceptable point supported with evidence.	2 (2e)

Set A: Grammar, Punctuation and Spelling Paper 1

Content Domain Coverage

The table below shows the aspects of grammar, punctuation and spelling assessed in Set A paper 1.

Qu.	Content domain reference	Mark
1	G1.2: Verbs	1
2	G5.3: Question marks	1
3	G5.4: Exclamation marks G5.7: Inverted commas	1
4	G1.6a: Adverbials	1
5	G5.8: Apostrophes	1
6	G1.6: Adverbs	1
7	G1.4: Conjunctions	1
8	G2.2: Questions	1
9	G2.1: Statements	1
10	G5.11: Semi-colons	1
11	G2.3: Commands	1
12	G5.14: Bullet points	1
13	G5.8: Apostrophes	1
14	G5.11: Semi-colons	1
15	G6.1: Synonyms and antonyms	1
16	G1.3: Adjectives	1
17	G4.1c: Modal verbs	1
18	G1.9: Subject and object	1
19	G2: Functions of sentences	1
20	G7.1: Standard English	1
21	G3.1a: Relative clauses	1
22	G1.3: Adjectives	1
23	G7: Standard English and formality	1
24	G4.1a: Simple past and simple present	1
25	G1.5a: Possessive pronouns	1
26	G5.1: Capital letters	1
27	G4.4: Passive and active	1
28	G1.4: Conjunctions	1

Qu.	Content domain reference	Mark
29a	G5.6a: Commas to clarify meaning	1
29b	G5.5: Commas in lists G5.6a: Commas to clarify meaning	1
30	G5.9: Punctuation for parenthesis	1
31	G1.5: Pronouns	1
32	G5.7: Inverted commas	1
33	G6.2: Prefixes	1
34	G5.12: Single dashes	1
35	G5.13: Hyphens	1
36	G1.5b: Relative pronouns	1
37	G5.9: Punctuation for parenthesis	1
38	G3.4: Subordinating conjunctions and subordinate clauses	1
39	G3.2: Noun phrases	1
40	G3.3: Co-ordinating conjunctions G3.4: Subordinating conjunctions and subordinate clauses	1
41	G1.8: Determiners	1
42	G3.2: Noun phrases	1
43	G4.1d: Present and past progressive	1
44	G1.3: Adjectives G1.6: Adverbs G1.7: Prepositions G1.8: Determiners	1
45	G6.4: Word families	1
46	G5.6a: Commas to clarify meaning	1
47	G5.5: Commas in lists	1
48	G5.2: Full stops	1
49	G7.4: The subjunctive	1

Set A: Grammar, Punctuation and Spelling Paper 1 – Answers

Qu.	Answer	Marking notes	Marks *(Domain)*
1	verb		**1** *(G1.2)*
2	"We're going to the restaurant, aren't we" asked Nikhil. ↑ ✓		**1** *(G5.3)*
3	"What an amazing house that is!" gasped Yasmin.		**1** *(G5.4 G5.7)*
4	After lunch		**1** *(G1.6a)*
5	cannot and should not	1 mark for both correct.	**1** *(G5.8)*
6	quite		**1** *(G1.6)*
7	He said that, <u>although</u> it is raining, we can go for a walk <u>after</u> we have eaten. I'd rather stay inside <u>or</u> go to the swimming pool.	1 mark for all 3 correct.	**1** *(G1.4)*

Qu.	Answer	Marking notes	Marks (Domain)
8	didn't I		1 (G2.2)
9	We should try to get tickets early. I told you to turn left at the end of the road.	1 mark for both correct.	1 (G2.1)
10	My auntie has bought a new house it's much bigger than her old one. ↑ ✓		1 (G5.11)
11	Unlock the gate.	1 mark for a grammatically correct command which is correctly punctuated.	1 (G2.3)
12	For his trip, Andrew needs to pack: • jeans • toothpaste • pyjamas • socks	1 mark for all 4 correct. If the answer uses capitalisation, it should do so at the start of each point. If the answer uses punctuation, it should use either commas or semi-colons after the first three points and a full stop after the fourth.	1 (G5.14)
13	mum's		1 (G5.8)
14	semi-colon		1 (G5.11)
15	suitable — appropriate; challenging — difficult; apparent — obvious; tedious — unexciting	1 mark for all 4 correct.	1 (G6.1)
16	new, playful and favourite	1 mark for all 3 correct.	1 (G1.3)
17	Dinner will be ready soon.		1 (G4.1c)
18	Chris congratulated <u>his team</u> after the rounders game. This morning, I ate <u>two apples</u>. We bought <u>a television</u> at the supermarket.	1 mark for all 3 correct. The mark should still be awarded if pupils have not underlined the objects' determiners.	1 (G1.9)
19	Plan the journey carefully — command; Will the journey be very long — question; The journey will last around six hours — statement; What a long journey we have had — exclamation	1 mark for all 4 correct.	1 (G2)
20	was, anything and that	1 mark for all 3 correct.	1 (G7.1)
21	Adam's suit which his mother bought him is hanging at the back of his wardrobe. ↑ ✓		1 (G3.1a)
22	If you are looking for an interesting hobby, you could learn a <u>musical</u> instrument. It can be very rewarding and will bring you <u>endless</u> enjoyment.	1 mark for both correct.	1 (G1.3)

Qu.	Answer	Marking notes	Marks *(Domain)*
23	The owner insisted that we remove our shoes. They had a superb painting on the wall.	1 mark for both correct.	**1** *(G7)*
24	sleep ——→ **slept** enjoy ——→ **enjoyed** swims ——→ **swam**	1 mark for all 3 correct. Answers must be spelt correctly.	**1** *(G4.1a)*
25	ours		**1** *(G1.5a)*
26	my, james, williams, he, manchester and saturday	1 mark for all 6 correct.	**1** *(G5.1)*
27	The charity buffet was arranged for Tuesday.		**1** *(G4.4)*
28	Before, and and if	1 mark for all 3 correct.	**1** *(G1.4)*
29a	After they paid Ryan, Lindsay and Jasmine went home.		**1** *(G5.6a)*
29b	After they paid, Ryan, Lindsay and Jasmine went home.	1 mark for both correct.	**1** *(G5.5 G5.6a)*
30	My cousins — Rachael and Phillip — will pick me up so we can go to the play.	1 mark for both correct.	**1** *(G5.9)*
31	They —— Anna and Diego (the cakes / the friends / Anna and Diego / the families)		**1** *(G1.5)*
32	Answers may vary, for example: He asked her, "Did you enjoy the film?" He asked her, "Would you say you enjoyed the film?"	1 mark for a grammatically correct question which is correctly punctuated using speech marks and a question mark in the appropriate places.	**1** *(G5.7)*
33	Answers may vary; accept any two suitable explanations, for example: Katie refilled the bucket. This means that the bucket was filled up again. Katie overfilled the bucket. This means that the bucket was filled until it was too full.	1 mark for both correct. Do not deduct marks for errors in spelling, punctuation and grammar.	**1** *(G6.2)*
34	Rebecca went into the dining room — it was extremely quiet.		**1** *(G5.12)*
35	We are getting a twelve-week-old kitten tomorrow.		**1** *(G5.13)*
36	that		**1** *(G1.5b)*
37	Amy, who lives near the coast, loves sailing.	1 mark for both correct.	**1** *(G5.9)*
38	Answers may vary, for example: Before she went swimming, Samantha went to the supermarket. Samantha went to the supermarket because she needed some milk.	1 mark for any sentence where a subordinate clause has been added correctly.	**1** *(G3.4)*
39	the old house next to the park		**1** *(G3.2)*

Qu.	Answer	Marking notes	Marks (Domain)
40	<table><tr><th>Sentence</th><th>Co-ordinating conjunction</th><th>Subordinating conjunction</th></tr><tr><td>**Until** we get a television, we won't be able to watch the matches.</td><td></td><td>✓</td></tr><tr><td>We are running out of kitchen roll, **so** we need to go to the shop.</td><td>✓</td><td></td></tr><tr><td>Anthony hates smoothies, **yet** he loves fruit juice.</td><td>✓</td><td></td></tr></table>	1 mark for all 3 correct.	1 (G3.3 G3.4)
41	three, the and any	1 mark for all 3 correct.	1 (G1.8)
42	a noun phrase		1 (G3.2)
43	The girls <u>are playing</u> a game of volleyball on the beach, and their brother <u>is swimming</u> in the sea.	1 mark for both correct. Answers must be spelt correctly.	1 (G4.1d)
44	A new boy started at my school today. He was very friendly. (A ↑) (C ↑) (D ↑) (B ↑)	1 mark for all 4 correct.	1 (G1.3 G1.6 G1.7 G1.8)
45	place		1 (G6.4)
46	The first sentence means that only cats that are often active at night make the best pets. The second sentence means that all cats make the best pets and are often active at night.	Do not deduct marks for errors in spelling, punctuation and grammar.	1 (G5.6a)
47	Answers may vary, for example: The shopping list includes a birthday card (for Dad), a loaf of bread, a pint of milk and self-raising flour. I need to buy several things: a birthday card (for Dad); a loaf of bread; a pint of milk; and self-raising flour.	1 mark for any suitable sentence which lists all the information and is punctuated correctly.	1 (G5.5)
48	full stop		1 (G5.2)
49	Their parents asked that they be careful.		1 (G7.4)

Set B: Grammar, Punctuation and Spelling Paper 1

Content Domain Coverage

The table below shows the aspects of grammar, punctuation and spelling assessed in Set B paper 1.

Qu.	Content domain reference	Mark
1	G1.3: Adjectives	1
2	G4.2: Tense consistency	1
3	G5.3: Question marks	1
4	G5.4: Exclamation marks	1
5	G5.2: Full stops	1
6	G1.4: Conjunctions	1
7	G4.1d: Present and past progressive	1
8	G2.1: Statements G2.3: Commands	1
9	G5.7: Inverted commas	1
10	G1.5a: Possessive pronouns	1
11	G5.8: Apostrophes	1
12	G5.6b: Commas after fronted adverbials	1
13	G7.1: Standard English	1
14	G7.2: Formal and informal vocabulary	1
15	G5.5: Commas in lists G5.9: Punctuation for parenthesis	1
16	G6.2: Prefixes	1
17	G4.1a: Simple past and simple present	1
18	G5.13: Hyphens	1
19	G4.1d: Present and past progressive	1
20	G1.4: Conjunctions	1
21	G1.7: Prepositions	1
22	G4.1c: Modal verbs	1
23	G1.2: Verbs G1.9: Subject and object	1
24	G1.1: Nouns G1.2: Verbs	2
25	G7.1: Standard English	1
26	G2.2: Questions	1

Qu.	Content domain reference	Mark
27	G5.7: Inverted commas	1
28	G5.12: Single dashes	1
29	G1.3: Adjectives G1.6: Adverbs	1
30	G1.6a: Adverbials	1
31a	G6.1: Synonyms and antonyms	1
31b	G6.1: Synonyms and antonyms	1
32	G5.10: Colons	1
33	G4.1b: Verbs in the perfect form	1
34	G1.5b: Relative pronouns	1
35	G1.8: Determiners	1
36	G3.1a: Relative clauses	1
37	G6.3: Suffixes	1
38	G3.2: Noun phrases	1
39	G1.6: Adverbs	1
40	G3.2: Noun phrases G3.4: Subordinating conjunctions and subordinate clauses	1
41	G5.9: Punctuation for parenthesis	1
42	G6.4: Word families	1
43	G4.4: Passive and active	1
44	G3.4: Subordinating conjunctions and subordinate clauses	1
45	G1.5a: Possessive pronouns	1
46	G1.7: Prepositions G3.4: Subordinating conjunctions and subordinate clauses	1
47	G4.3: Subjunctive verb forms	1
48	G5.6b: Commas after fronted adverbials G5.9: Punctuation for parenthesis	1

Set B: Grammar, Punctuation and Spelling Paper 1 – Answers

Qu.	Answer	Marking notes	Marks (Domain)
1	adjective		1 (G1.3)
2	were are		1 (G4.2)
3	?		1 (G5.3)

4	"How fantastic that is" cried Alex, running over to hug Shahnaz.
	        ↑
	        ☑
			1
			(G5.4)

5	I got a new bike today. It's red and white with a basket on the front so I can carry things.		1 (G5.2)
6	My brother and I needed to clean our bedrooms <u>before</u> going to the party. I did the vacuuming <u>while</u> my brother made the beds. We were pleased <u>that</u> we finished in time.	1 mark for all 3 correct.	1 (G1.4)

Qu.	Answer	Marking notes	Marks (Domain)
7	She is tidying her bedroom.		1 (G4.1d)
8	<table><tr><th>Sentence</th><th>Statement</th><th>Command</th></tr><tr><td>I asked if I could open my present.</td><td>✓</td><td></td></tr><tr><td>Don't spend too much money on the present.</td><td></td><td>✓</td></tr><tr><td>She might buy me a present.</td><td>✓</td><td></td></tr></table>	1 mark for all 3 correct.	1 (G2.1 G2.3)
9	Susan said, "We need to leave as early as possible."		1 (G5.7)
10	hers his		1 (G1.5a)
11	Were, Dads and cant	1 mark for all 3 correct.	1 (G5.8)
12	Smiling widely, Jenny handed Chris the fluffy puppy.		1 (G5.6b)
13	slowly, those and isn't	1 mark for all 3 correct.	1 (G7.1)
14	Answers may vary, for example: threw cast	1 mark for any suitable formal synonym.	1 (G7.2)
15	Rachel, Frances and Rosie, who lives next door, came to the party.	1 mark for all 3 correct.	1 (G5.5 G5.9)
16	im — possible un — able over — react	1 mark for all 3 correct.	1 (G6.2)
17	was and walked	1 mark for both correct.	1 (G4.1a)
18	hyphen		1 (G5.13)
19	<table><tr><th>Sentence</th><th>Present progressive</th><th>Past progressive</th></tr><tr><td>Jack was baking a cake for two hours.</td><td></td><td>✓</td></tr><tr><td>Jack is planning to open his own bakery.</td><td>✓</td><td></td></tr><tr><td>Jack's cakes are baking in the oven right now.</td><td>✓</td><td></td></tr></table>	1 mark for all 3 correct.	1 (G4.1d)
20	since, or and because	1 mark for all 3 correct.	1 (G1.4)
21	I have a clarinet lesson after school. My scooter is in the garden shed. They had some decorations above the door.	1 mark for all 3 correct.	1 (G1.7)
22	Sophie will sit next to me on the bus. They could complete the journey in two hours.	1 mark for both correct.	1 (G4.1c)

23	Riyad knits cardigans.
	  ↑ ↑ ↑
	  S V O
		1 mark for all 3 correct.	1 (G1.2 G1.9)

Qu.	Answer	Marking notes	Marks *(Domain)*
24	Verb — answers may vary, for example: To get to the school, turn right after the mosque. Noun — answers may vary, for example: It was Chris's turn to do the washing up. **Do not accept** answers in which the given word has been changed.	1 mark per suitable sentence. Sentences must be grammatically correct, punctuated correctly and contain a verb or noun as appropriate.	**2** *(G1.1 G1.2)*
25	The error is 'was'. The correct word is 'were'.	1 mark if 'was' is circled and 'were' is written in the box.	**1** *(G7.1)*
26	Answers may vary, for example: <table><tr><th>Statement</th><th>Question</th></tr><tr><td>She plays the piano.</td><td><u>Does she play the piano?</u></td></tr></table>	1 mark for a grammatically correct sentence which is correctly punctuated using a capital letter and a question mark.	**1** *(G2.2)*
27	"Wait a minute,<u>"</u> Dad called. <u>"</u>Don't forget to take your jacket.<u>"</u>	1 mark for all 3 correct.	**1** *(G5.7)*

28	We couldn't get her the new necklace it was too expensive.
	               ↑
	             ✓
			1
			(G5.12)

29	<table><tr><th>Sentence</th><th>Adjective</th><th>Adverb</th></tr><tr><td>He put the vase down **carefully**.</td><td></td><td>✓</td></tr><tr><td>We sat in the **chilly** living room.</td><td>✓</td><td></td></tr><tr><td>Her new curtains are **lovely**.</td><td>✓</td><td></td></tr><tr><td>They arrived **late** for the flight.</td><td></td><td>✓</td></tr></table>	1 mark for all 4 correct.	**1** *(G1.3 G1.6)*
30	This evening, we are going to a barbecue.		**1** *(G1.6a)*
31a	Answers may vary, for example: A word that means the opposite or nearly the opposite of another word.	Do not deduct marks for errors in spelling, punctuation and grammar.	**1** *(G6.1)*
31b	Answers may vary, for example: careless sloppy		**1** *(G6.1)*
32	Ben was tired: he hadn't slept very well.		**1** *(G5.10)*
33	had been		**1** *(G4.1b)*
34	who		**1** *(G1.5b)*
35	some, the and four	1 mark for all 3 correct.	**1** *(G1.8)*
36	that she had owned since birth		**1** *(G3.1a)*
37	Answers may vary, for example: delight ⟶ **delightful / delighted** worth ⟶ **worthy / worthless** option ⟶ **optional**	1 mark for all 3 correct.	**1** *(G6.3)*

Qu.	Answer	Marking notes	Marks (Domain)
38	Answers may vary; accept any suitable noun phrase, for example: 	Noun	Noun phrase
---	---
the curtains	the old curtains in the dining room
the skateboard	the small skateboard in the cupboard		1 mark for any answer that creates a noun phrase by adding words both before and after the noun. Do not deduct marks for misspellings.	**1** (G3.2)
39	confidently and also	1 mark for both correct.	**1** (G1.6)
40		Sentence	Noun phrase	Subordinate clause
---	---	---
My brother's best friend has a holiday home in Spain.	✓	
Even if we get the last bus, we will still be on time for the play.		✓
We can't watch the film **until we fix the DVD player.**		✓		1 mark for all 3 correct.	**1** (G3.2 G3.4)
41	Answers may vary, for example: Brackets have been used to add extra information to the sentence. Brackets have been used for parenthesis.	1 mark for answers that offer any valid explanation that refers to the use of brackets for parenthesis or to add extra information. Do not deduct marks for errors in spelling, punctuation and grammar.	**1** (G5.9)
42	new		**1** (G6.4)
43	Answers may vary, for example: The garage repaired my car. The garage has repaired my car.	1 mark for an answer correctly written in the active voice.	**1** (G4.4)
44	rather than		**1** (G3.4)
45	Answers may vary, for example: mine hers theirs	1 mark for any possessive pronoun.	**1** (G1.5a)
46		Sentence	Preposition	Subordinating conjunction
---	---	---
After we'd been to the concert, we had dinner at a restaurant.		✓
I won't go there again **after** such a terrible experience.	✓	
We will give the tent back to him **after** we return from the trip.		✓		1 mark for all 3 correct.	**1** (G1.7 G3.4)
47	were		**1** (G4.3)
48	Next week, my cousin, who loves travelling, is going to Paris.		**1** (G5.6b G5.9)

Grammar, Punctuation and Spelling Paper 2

Content Domain Coverage

Set A: Spelling

The table below shows the aspects of spelling assessed in Set A paper 2.

Qu.	Spelling	Content domain reference	Mark
1	opening	S38 — adding suffixes beginning with vowel letters to words of more than one syllable	1
2	commonly	S43 — the suffix -ly	1
3	crumb	S60 — words with 'silent' letters	1
4	piece	S61 — homophones and near homophones	1
5	suffering	S57 — adding suffixes beginning with vowel letters to words ending in –fer	1
6	disloyal	S41 — prefixes	1
7	construction	S47 — endings that sound like 'shun', spelt -tion, -sion, -ssion, -cian	1
8	horrible	S56 — words ending in -able and -ible, words ending in -ably and -ibly	1
9	temptation	S42 — the suffix -ation	1
10	absence	S55 — words ending in -ant, -ance, -ancy, -ent, -ence, -ency	1
11	eighth	S52 — words with the 'ay' sound spelt ei, eigh, or ey	1
12	cautious	S53 — endings which sound like 'shus', spelt -cious or -tious	1
13	confusion	S45 — endings that sound like 'zhun'	1
14	courage	S40 — the 'u' sound spelt ou	1
15	vacancy	S55 — words ending in -ant, -ance, -ancy, -ent, -ence, -ency	1
16	mechanic	S48 — words with the 'k' sound spelt ch	1
17	glorious	S46 — the suffix -ous	1
18	cylinder	S39 — the 'i' sound spelt y other than at the end of words	1
19	confidential	S54 — endings which sound like 'shul'	1
20	musician	S47 — endings that sound like 'shun', spelt -tion, -sion, -ssion, -cian	1

Set B: Spelling

The table below shows the aspects of spelling assessed in Set B paper 2.

Qu.	Spelling	Content domain reference	Mark
1	mismatch	S41 — prefixes	1
2	bury	S61 — homophones and near homophones	1
3	young	S40 — the 'u' sound spelt ou	1
4	forgotten	S38 — adding suffixes beginning with vowel letters to words of more than one syllable	1
5	pleasant	S55 — words ending in -ant, -ance, -ancy, -ent, -ence, -ency	1
6	chemist	S48 — words with the 'k' sound spelt ch	1
7	envious	S46 — the suffix -ous	1
8	selection	S47 — endings that sound like 'shun', spelt -tion, -sion, -ssion, -cian	1
9	through	S59 — words containing the letter string ough	1
10	vague	S50 — words ending with the 'g' sound spelt -gue and the 'k' sound spelt -que	1
11	flour	S61 — homophones and near homophones	1
12	descent	S51 — words with the 's' sound spelt sc	1
13	irrelevant	S41 — prefixes	1
14	permission	S47 — endings that sound like 'shun', spelt -tion, -sion, -ssion, -cian	1
15	unreasonably	S56 — words ending in -able and -ible, words ending in -ably and -ibly	1
16	received	S58 — words with the 'ee' sound spelt ei after c	1
17	enclosure	S44 — words with endings sounding like 'zhuh' and 'chuh'	1
18	invasion	S45 — endings that sound like 'zhun'	1
19	tremendous	S46 — the suffix -ous	1
20	malicious	S53 — endings which sound like 'shus', spelt -cious or -tious	1

Guidance for Marking the Spelling Task

Here's some guidance for marking the paper 2 spelling tests:

- If the pupil makes more than one attempt, it needs to be clear which answer they wish to be marked. If the pupil makes two or more attempts and it isn't clear which is to be considered, the mark should not be awarded.

- Pupils can answer in lower or upper case, or a mixture of the two. This is not the case for days of the week and months of the year — these must be written in lower-case letters with an initial capital letter.

- If the pupil has answered with the correct sequence of letters but has incorrectly inserted an apostrophe or a hyphen, the mark should not be awarded.

- If the pupil has answered with the correct sequence of letters but these have been separated into clearly divided components, with or without a hyphen, the mark should not be awarded.

Instructions for the Spelling Task

Each test should take about 15 minutes to do. This isn't a strict limit, so you can allow more time if needed.

Read out the following instructions, and answer any questions the children may have.

- *Listen to the instructions I'm about to give you.*
- *I'm going to read out twenty sentences. These sentences are printed in your answer booklet, but each one has a word missing. Listen to the missing word and write it in. Make sure you spell it correctly.*
- *I will read the word, then read the word within a sentence, then I'll say the word a third time.*
- *Have you got any questions?*

Now read the spellings to the children:

- Say the spelling number
- Say "*The word is...*"
- Read out the word in its sentence.
- Say "*The word is...*"
- Pause for at least 12 seconds between each of the spellings.

At the end of the test, read out all 20 sentences again, and give the children time to change their answers if they want to.

When the test is over, say "This is the end of the test."

Set A: Spelling – Script

Spelling one — the word is **opening**. *She tried to help him by **opening** the door.* The word is **opening**.

Spelling two — the word is **commonly**. *Squirrels are **commonly** found in forests.* The word is **commonly**.

Spelling three — the word is **crumb**. *There wasn't a single **crumb** left on the plate.* The word is **crumb**.

Spelling four — the word is **piece**. *Angela had another **piece** of pizza.* The word is **piece**.

Spelling five — the word is **suffering**. *She was **suffering** from a cold all week.* The word is **suffering**.

Spelling six — the word is **disloyal**. *They all agreed that he had been very **disloyal**.* The word is **disloyal**.

Spelling seven — the word is **construction**. *The building's **construction** took a long time.* The word is **construction**.

Spelling eight — the word is **horrible**. *The weather had been **horrible** all summer.* The word is **horrible**.

Spelling nine — the word is **temptation**. *He resisted the **temptation** to open the present.* The word is **temptation**.

Spelling ten — the word is **absence**. *The doctor wrote an **absence** note for her.* The word is **absence**.

Spelling eleven — the word is **eighth**. *It was the **eighth** time we had visited them.* The word is **eighth**.

Spelling twelve — the word is **cautious**. *He is a **cautious** person — he does not take risks.* The word is **cautious**.

Spelling thirteen — the word is **confusion**. *There was some **confusion** about where we were meeting.* The word is **confusion**.

Spelling fourteen — the word is **courage**. *It took a lot of **courage** to perform at the concert.* The word is **courage**.

Spelling fifteen — the word is **vacancy**. *My uncle applied for the job **vacancy** at the factory.* The word is **vacancy**.

Spelling sixteen — the word is **mechanic**. *He took the car to a professional **mechanic**.* The word is **mechanic**.

Spelling seventeen — the word is **glorious**. *Their balcony gave them a **glorious** view of the sea.* The word is **glorious**.

Spelling eighteen — the word is **cylinder**. *Mum's favourite vase was a **cylinder** shape.* The word is **cylinder**.

Spelling nineteen — the word is **confidential**. *They had a **confidential** meeting with the head teacher.* The word is **confidential**.

Spelling twenty — the word is **musician**. *Alex had a successful career as a **musician**.* The word is **musician**.

Set B: Spelling – Script

Spelling one — the word is **mismatch**. *He was careful not to **mismatch** his socks.* The word is **mismatch**.

Spelling two — the word is **bury**. *The dog wanted to **bury** its bone.* The word is **bury**.

Spelling three — the word is **young**. *The **young** woman shook the man's hand.* The word is **young**.

Spelling four — the word is **forgotten**. *Abdullah had **forgotten** to buy a ticket.* The word is **forgotten**.

Spelling five — the word is **pleasant**. *They had a **pleasant** morning by the pool.* The word is **pleasant**.

Spelling six — the word is **chemist**. *She bought some plasters from the **chemist**.* The word is **chemist**.

Spelling seven — the word is **envious**. *Sophie felt very **envious** of Mo's new bike.* The word is **envious**.

Spelling eight — the word is **selection**. *The assistant showed them a **selection** of colours.*
The word is **selection**.

Spelling nine — the word is **through**. *They had to walk **through** deep water to get back to the car.*
The word is **through**.

Spelling ten — the word is **vague**. *His description of the location was **vague**.* The word is **vague**.

Spelling eleven — the word is **flour**. *They needed some **flour** to bake the bread.* The word is **flour**.

Spelling twelve — the word is **descent**. *The **descent** from the mountain was tiring.* The word is **descent**.

Spelling thirteen — the word is **irrelevant**. *She made some **irrelevant** comments.* The word is **irrelevant**.

Spelling fourteen — the word is **permission**. *He gave them **permission** to look around his house.*
The word is **permission**.

Spelling fifteen — the word is **unreasonably**. *He acted **unreasonably** during the argument.*
The word is **unreasonably**.

Spelling sixteen — the word is **received**. *The girl **received** several gifts for her birthday.*
The word is **received**.

Spelling seventeen — the word is **enclosure**. *We visited the lion **enclosure** at the zoo.*
The word is **enclosure**.

Spelling eighteen — the word is **invasion**. *The army was planning an **invasion**.* The word is **invasion**.

Spelling nineteen — the word is **tremendous**. *The children made a **tremendous** amount of noise.*
The word is **tremendous**.

Spelling twenty — the word is **malicious**. *He didn't mean to be **malicious**.* The word is **malicious**.

CGP

Key Stage Two
SATS Practice Papers

This superb pack from CGP is overflowing with the most realistic
SATs practice you'll find, all fully up to date for the latest tests!

It contains two full sets of Practice Papers each for Maths and English, plus answers
and mark schemes — ideal for seeing where pupils need most practice.

As an extra treat, we've also thrown in some free online goodies — including
a Parents' Guide, Online Editions, pupil-friendly answers <u>and</u> quizzes!

How to access your free Online Extras

This pack includes free Online Extras to access on your PC, Mac or tablet.
You'll just need to go to **cgpbooks.co.uk/extras** and enter this code:

2185 8816 1109 2174

By the way, this code only works for one person. If somebody else has used
this book before you, they might have already claimed the Online Extras.

What CGP is all about

Our sole aim here at CGP is to produce the highest quality books —
carefully written, immaculately presented and
dangerously close to being funny.

Then we work our socks off to get them out to you
— at the cheapest possible prices.

Key Stage Two Mathematics

Set A
Paper 1: Arithmetic

Calculator Not Allowed

30 minutes

First name	
Middle name	
Last name	
School	

Date of birth	Day		Month		Year	

Total marks

Exam Set MHP26

1 5041 − 100 =

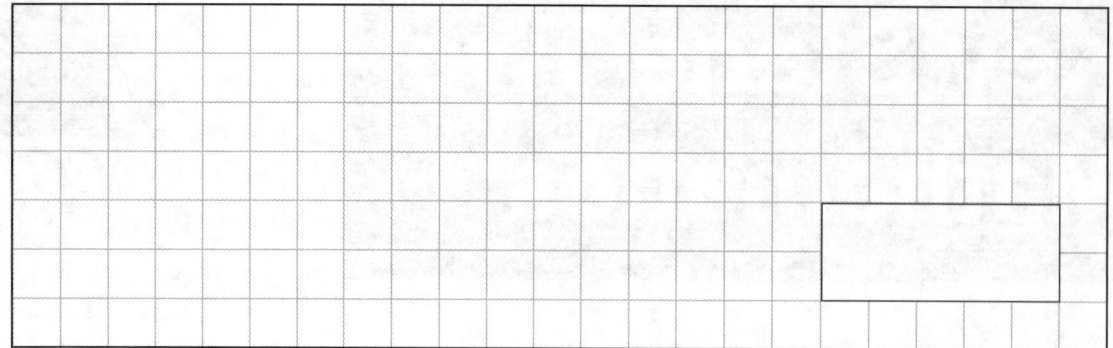

1 mark

2 74 × 2 =

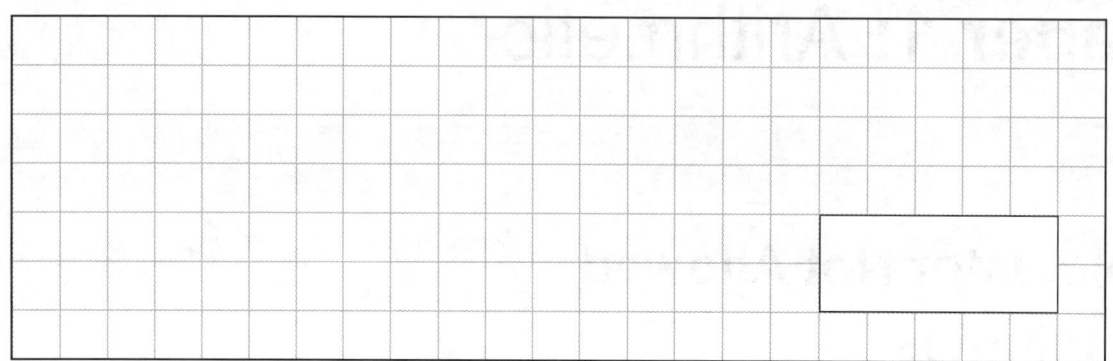

1 mark

3 ⬚ = 372 − 8

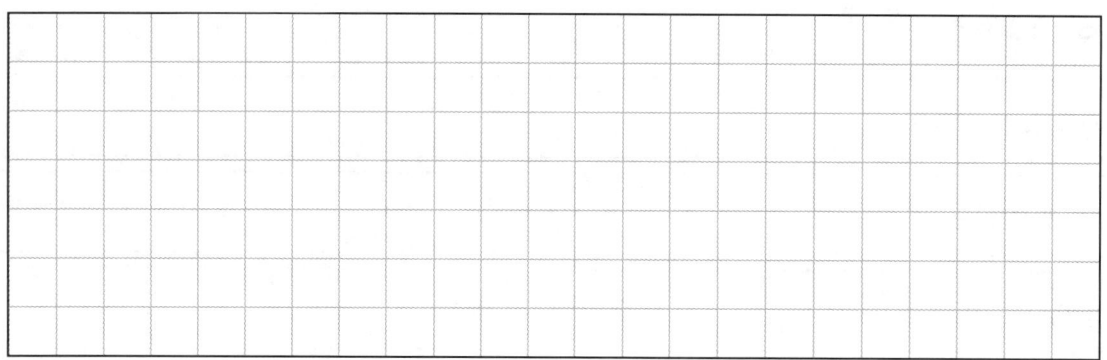

1 mark

4 44 ÷ 4 =

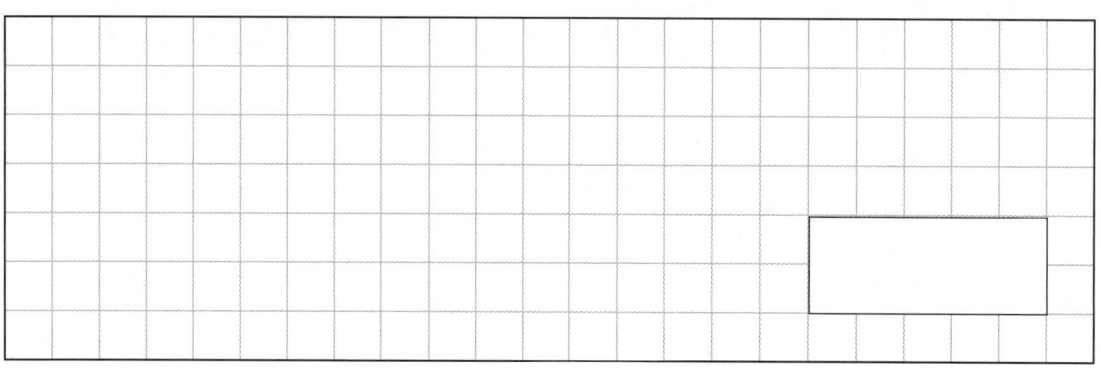

1 mark

5 730 ÷ 1 =

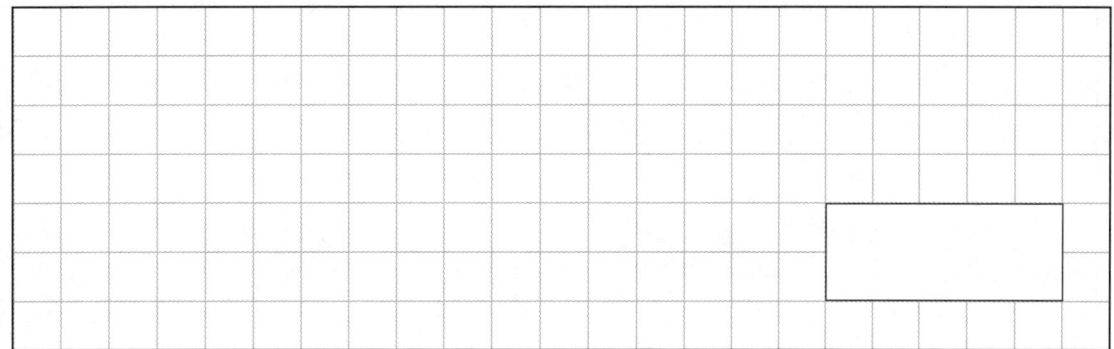

1 mark

6 8 × 5 × 6 =

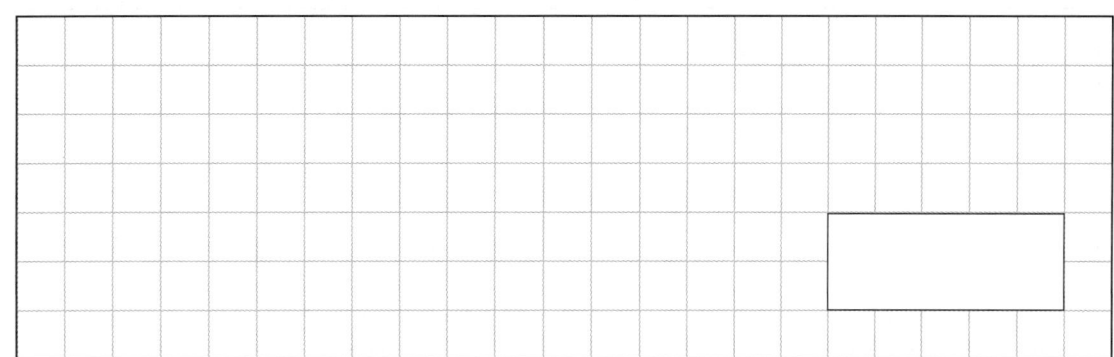

1 mark

7 76 985 + 5236 =

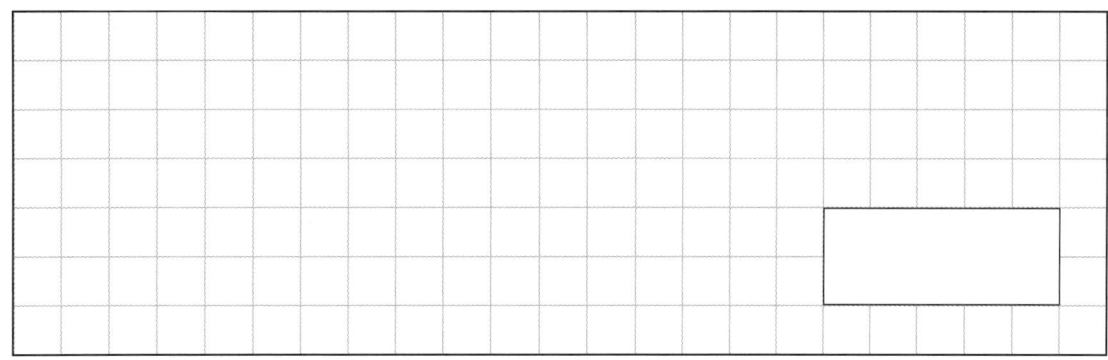

1 mark

8 9 × 25 =

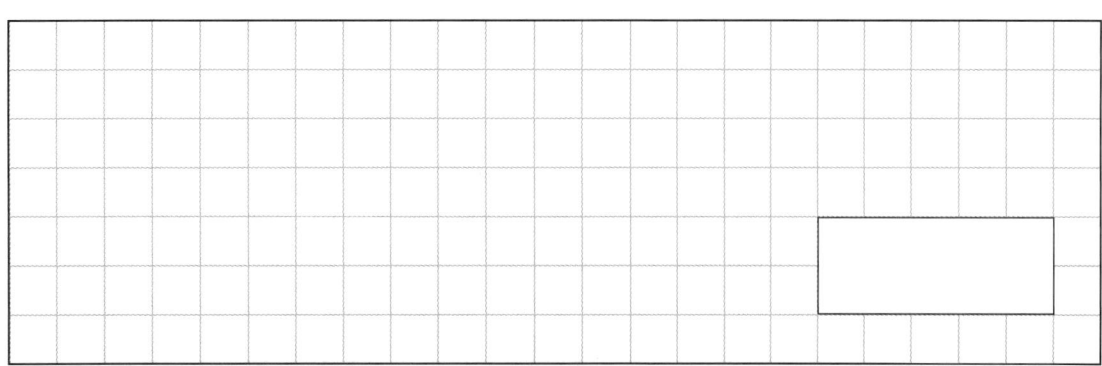

1 mark

9 40 × 40 =

1 mark

10 865 − 70 =

1 mark

11 ⬜ = 866 × 100

1 mark

12 546 × 4 =

1 mark

13 $73 \times 9 =$

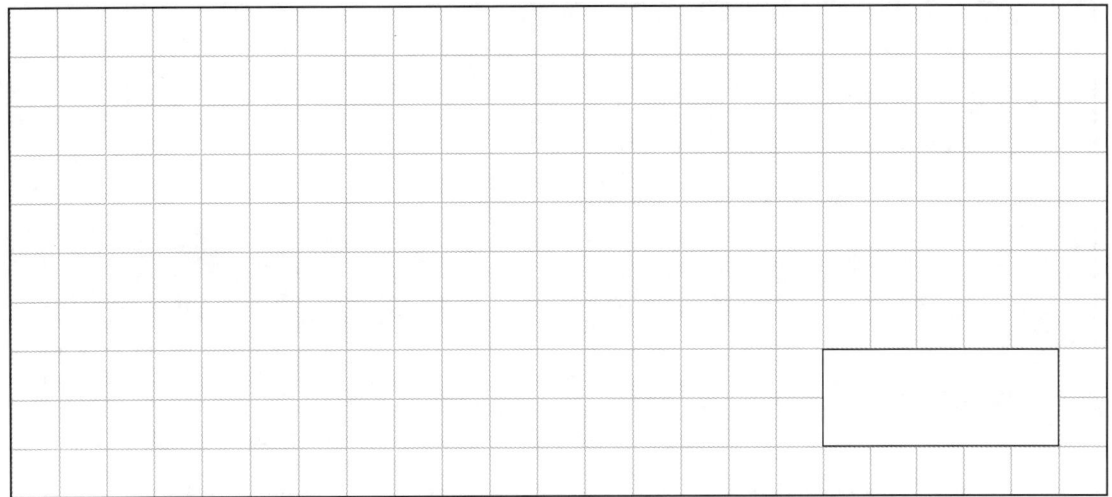

1 mark

14 $7.65 - 6.54 =$

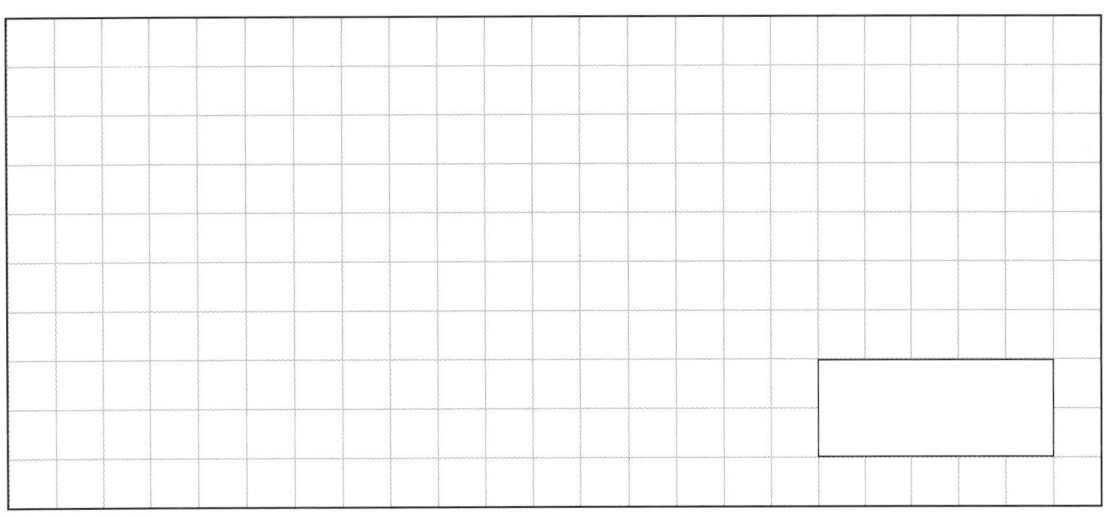

1 mark

15 $9.46 + 13.777 =$

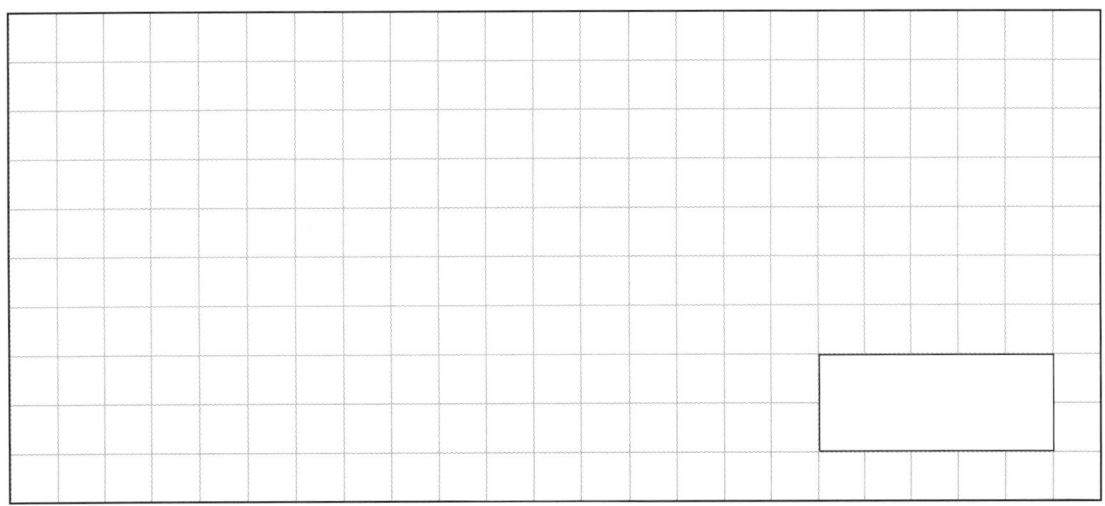

1 mark

16   77 000 − 707 =

1 mark

17   5474 ÷ 7 =

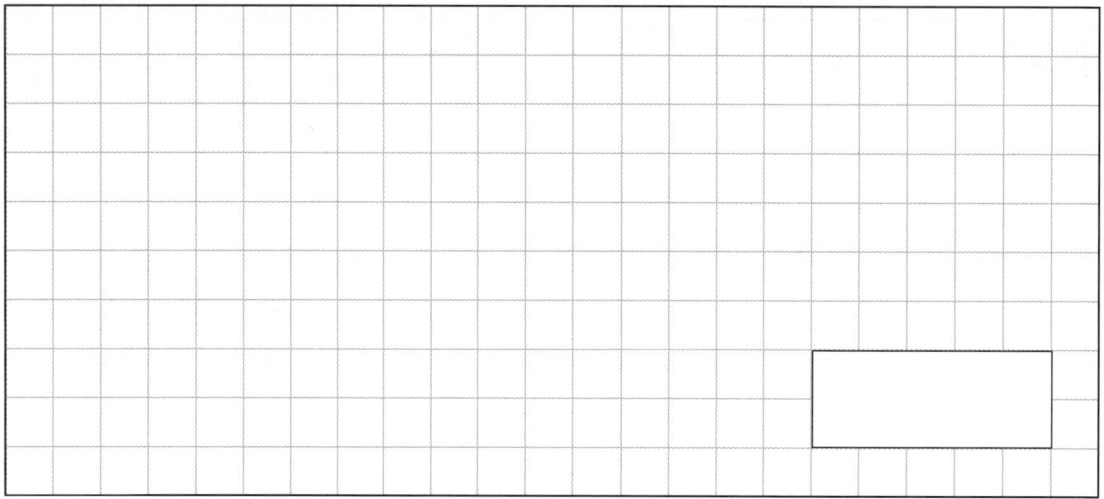

1 mark

18 $\frac{2}{7} + \frac{4}{7} =$

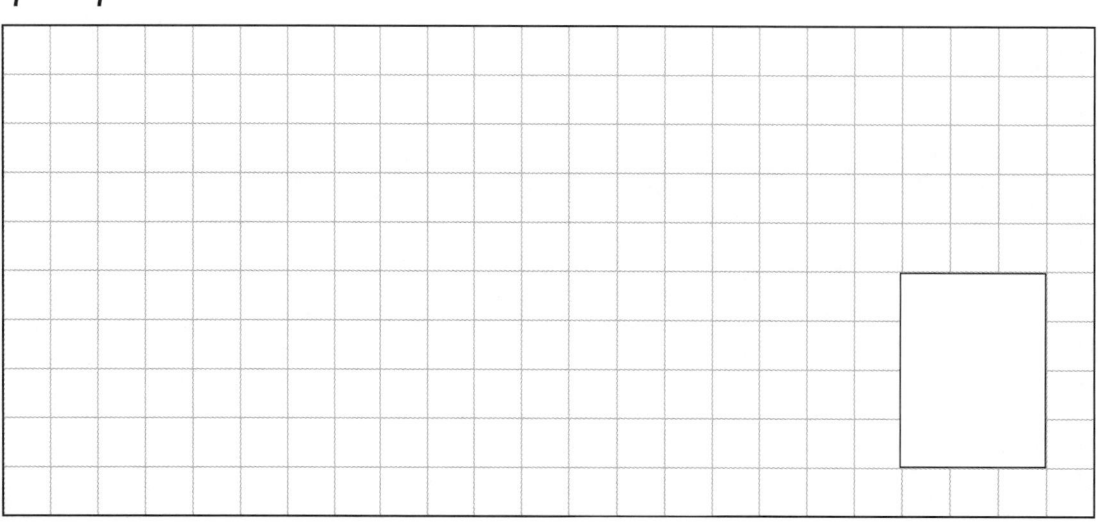

1 mark

19   55 – 5.72 =

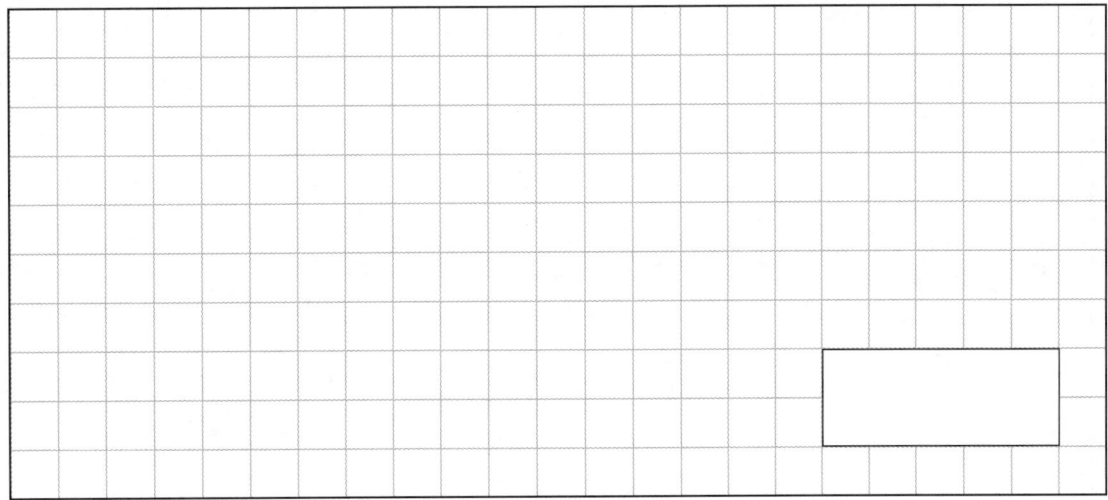

20   569 898 – 70 919 =

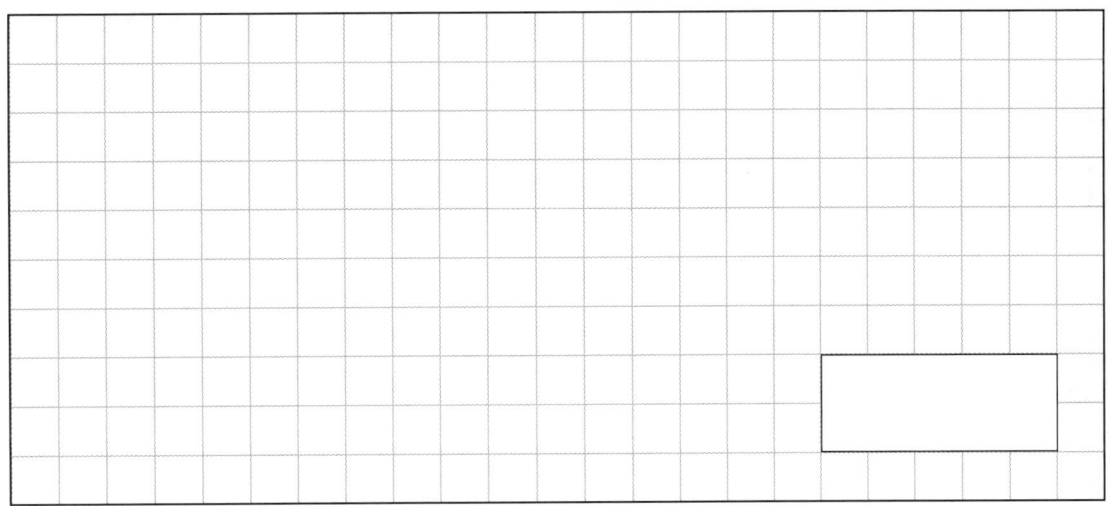

21   1.5 ÷ 1000 =

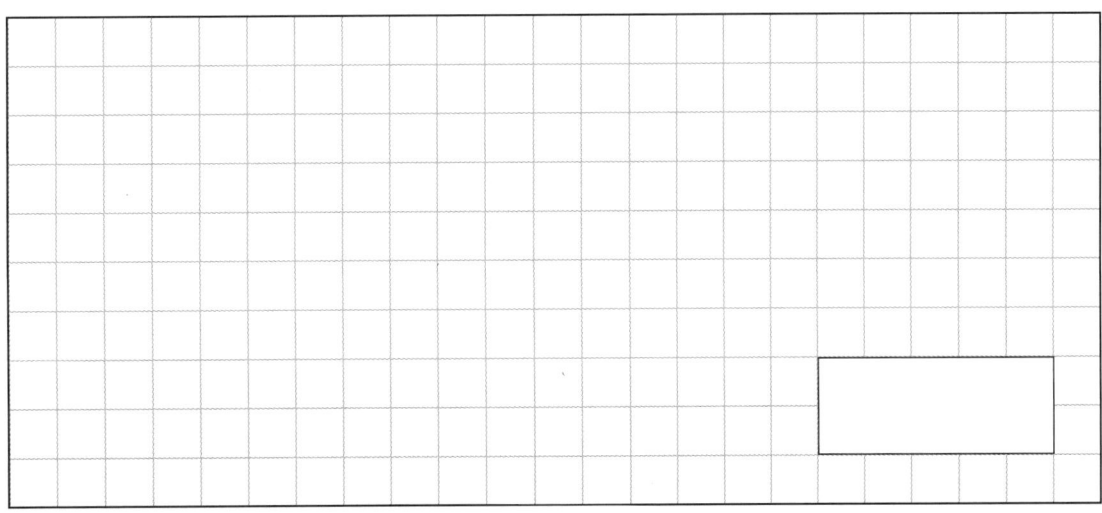

KS2 Maths / Set A / Paper 1

22 $2^3 + 2 =$

1 mark

23 $2310 \div 11 =$

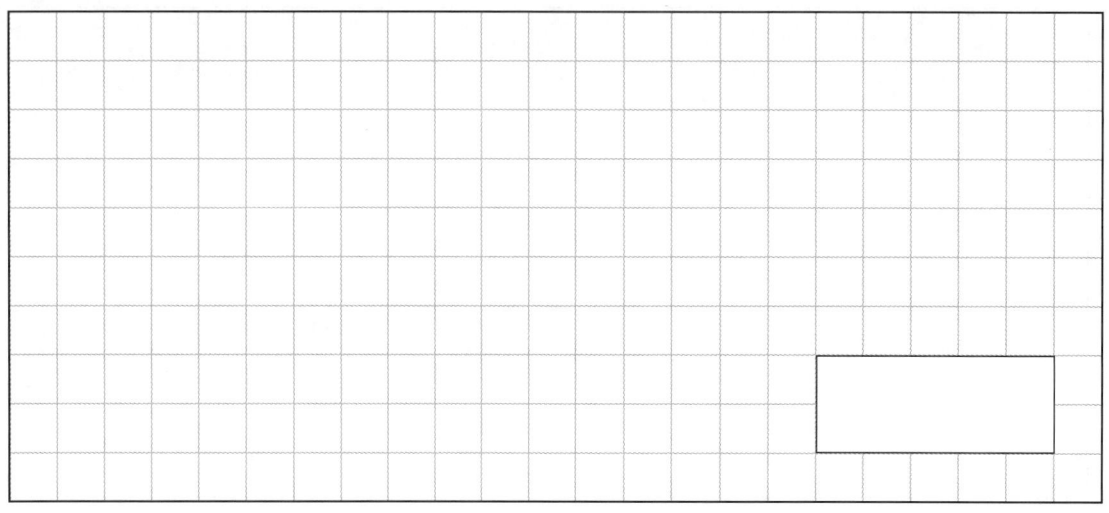

1 mark

24 $12 \times 7.4 =$

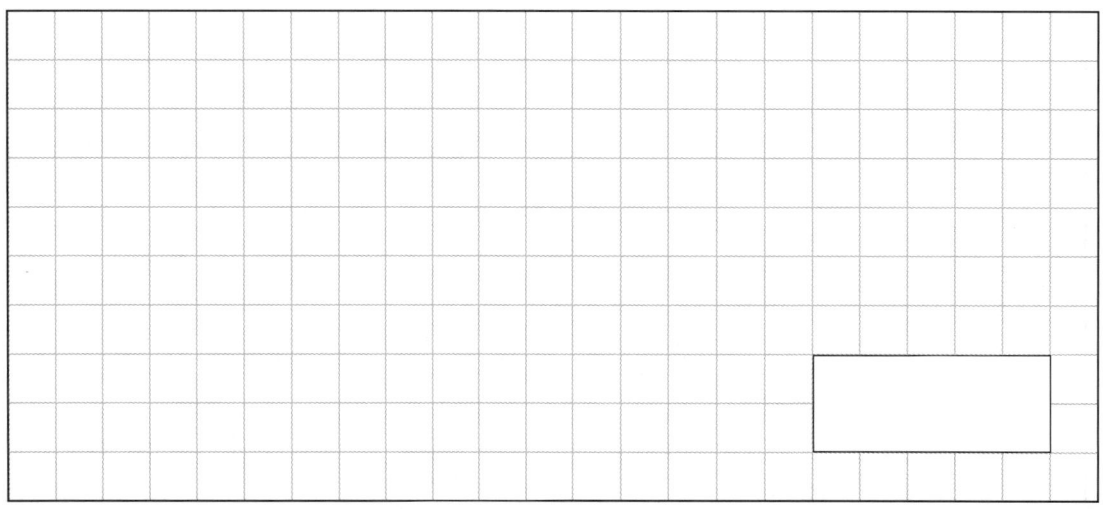

1 mark

25

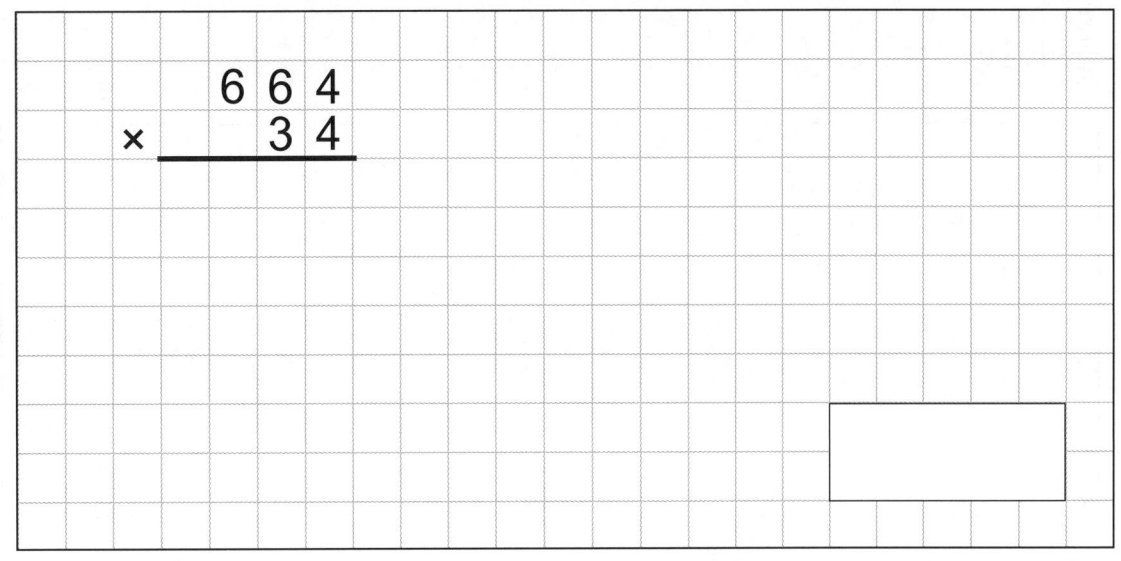

Show your working

2 marks

26 20% of 2400 =

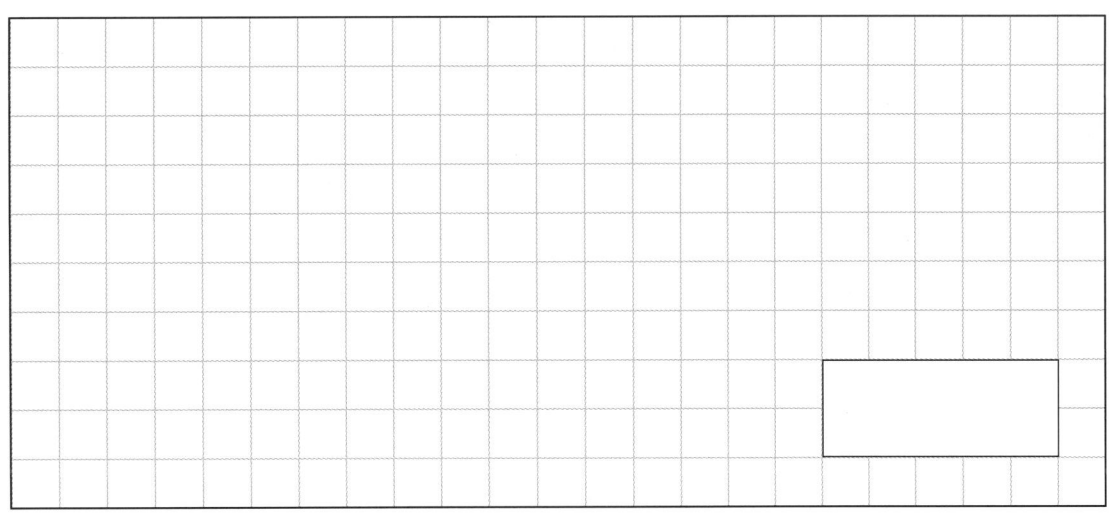

1 mark

27

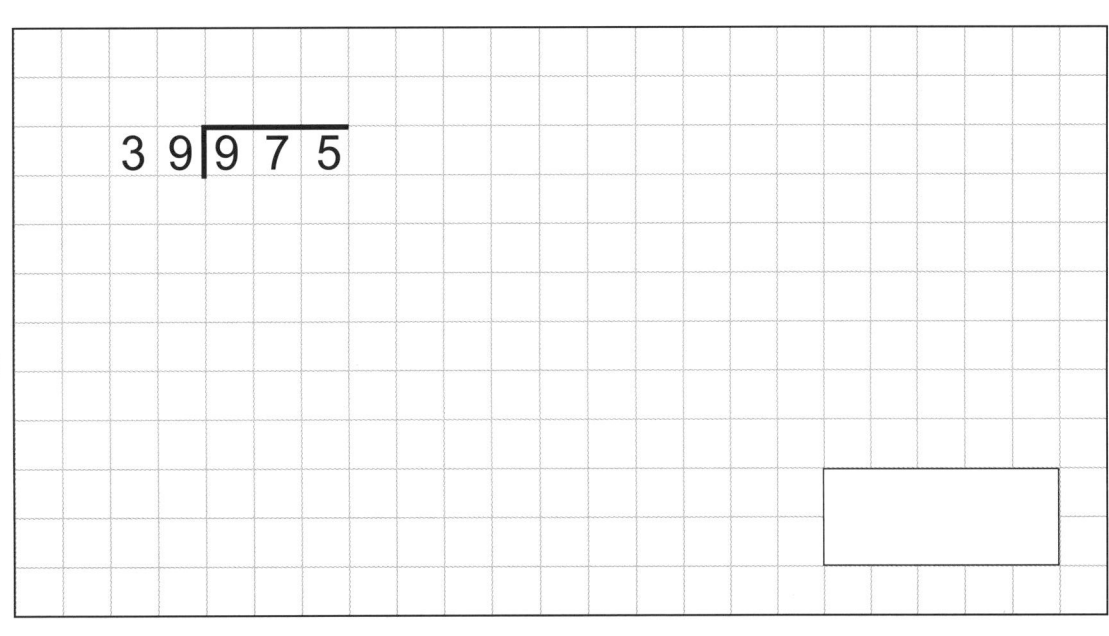

Show your working

2 marks

28 $\dfrac{5}{6} + 1\dfrac{1}{12} =$

1 mark

29 16.253 − 7.36 =

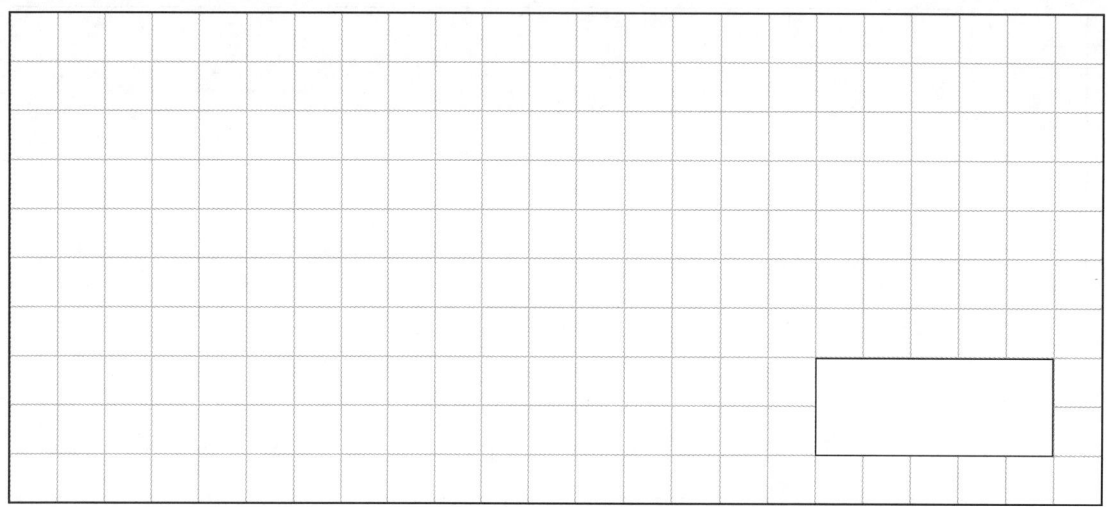

1 mark

30

Show
your
working

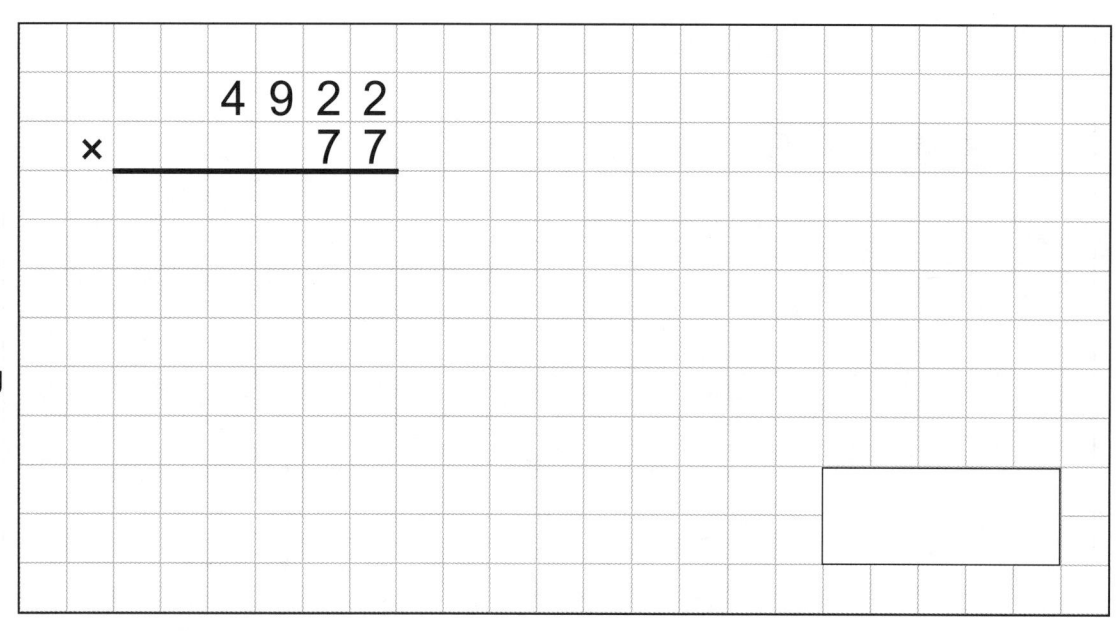

$$\begin{array}{r} 4\ 9\ 2\ 2 \\ \times\quad 7\ 7 \\ \hline \end{array}$$

2 marks

31 $22\% \times 350 =$

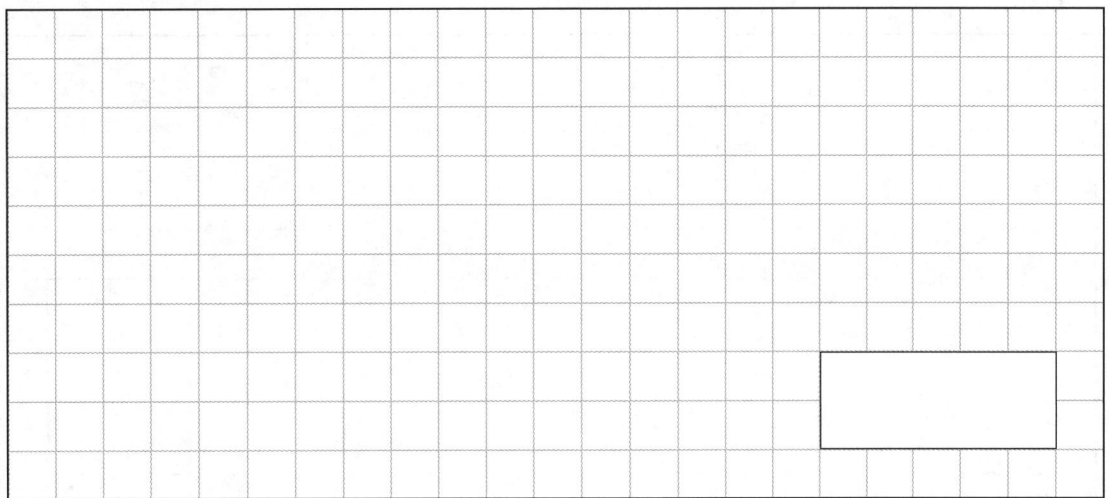

1 mark

32 $\dfrac{1}{2} \times \dfrac{2}{3} =$

1 mark

33

Show your working

$4\,5\,\lfloor\,6\,8\,8\,5$

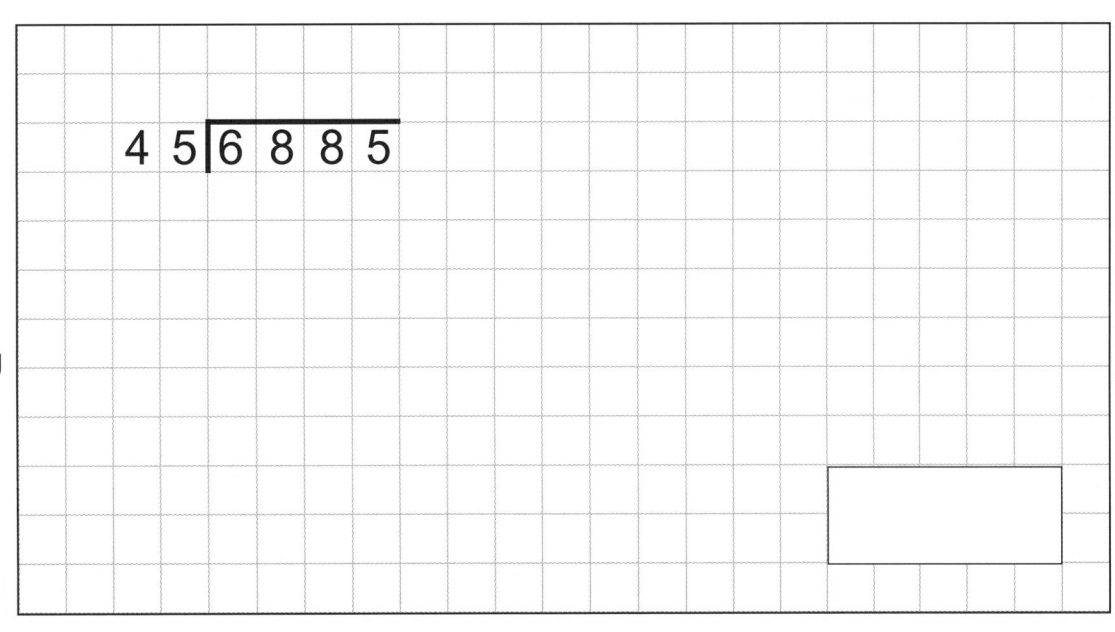

2 marks

34

$$\frac{7}{10} \div 9 =$$

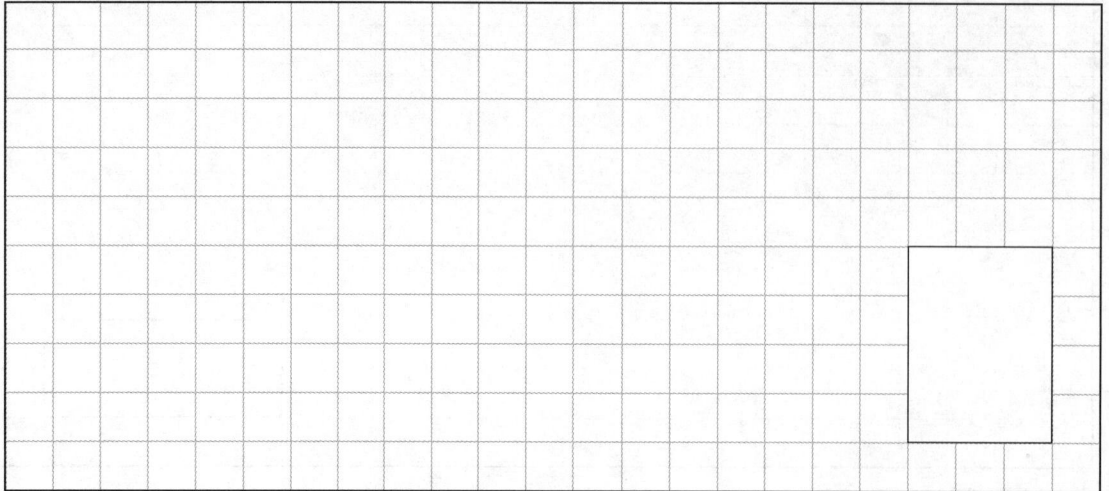

1 mark

35

$$\frac{1}{4} + \frac{4}{5} =$$

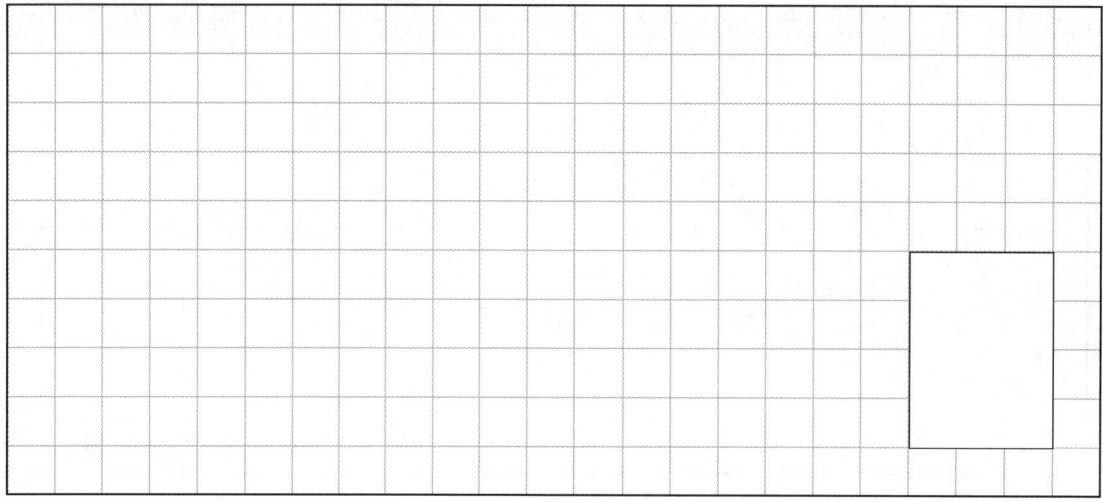

1 mark

36

$$44 + 72 \div 12 =$$

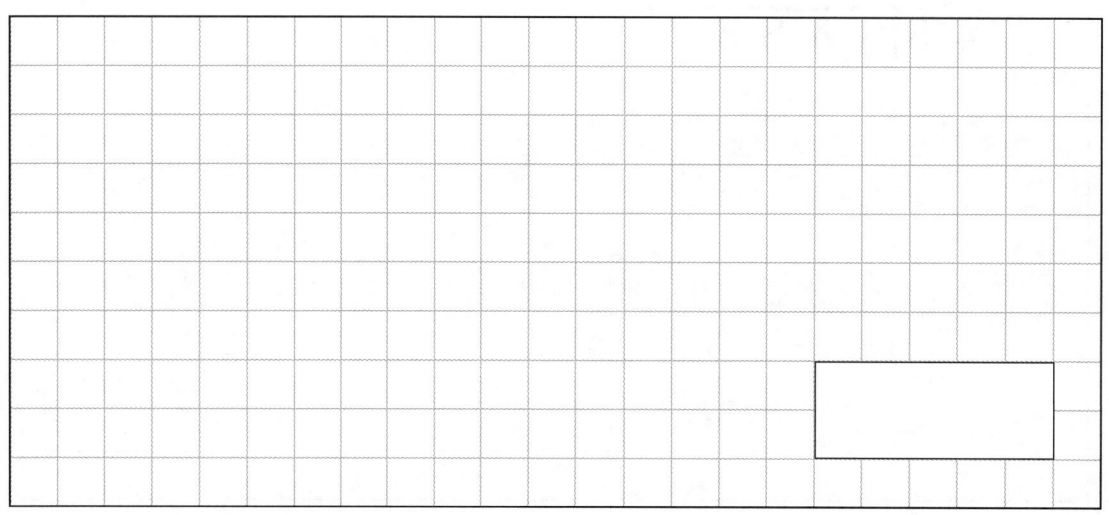

1 mark

MHP26U

Key Stage Two Mathematics

Set A
Paper 2: Reasoning

Calculator Not Allowed

40 minutes

First name	
Middle name	
Last name	
School	

Date of birth	Day		Month		Year	

Total marks

1 Draw the line of symmetry of this shape.

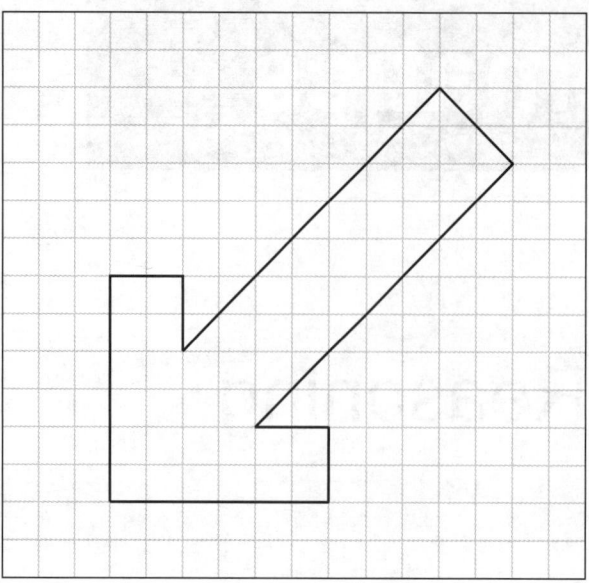

Draw **one** more square on the grid to give this shape a line of symmetry.

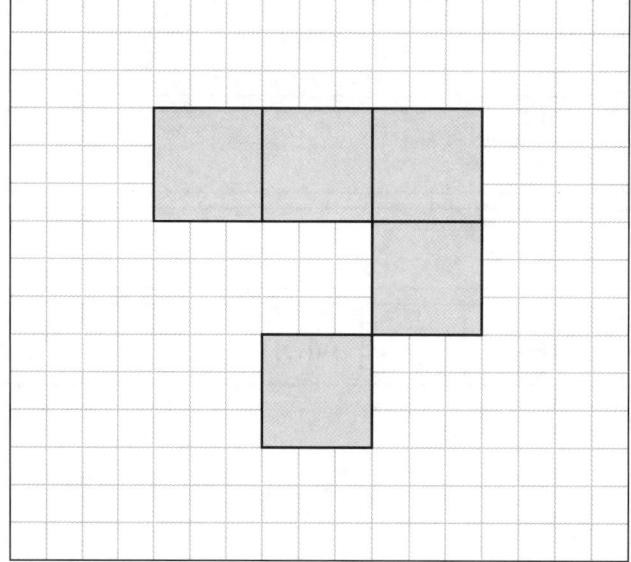

2 David needs 120 slices of bread to make sandwiches for a party.
He buys 6 loaves of bread.
Each loaf contains 22 slices.

How many slices are **left over** after David has made the sandwiches?

Show
your
working

| slices |

2 marks

3 At 9 am there were **12 ml** of rainwater in this measuring cylinder.
The diagram shows the cylinder at 4 pm on the same day.

How much rain fell into the cylinder between 9 am and 4 pm?

| ml |

1 mark

6 ml of rain fell between 4 pm and 8 pm.

Draw a line on the cylinder to show
the amount of water in the cylinder at 8 pm.

1 mark

4 This table shows the prize money in a lottery.

March	April	May	June
£7 651 302	£7 648 999	£6 988 256	£7 651 298

Write the months in order of their prize money, starting with the month with the **largest** prize.

largest   smallest

1 mark

5 A game has two rounds.
The table shows the scores that three children got in each round.

	Round 1	Round 2
Tom	-2	1
Aziza	-1	0
Billy	3	-1

Who got the **lowest** score in round 1?

1 mark

What is the **difference** between the scores Billy got in round 1 and round 2?

1 mark

Fill in the missing numbers to make the calculation correct.

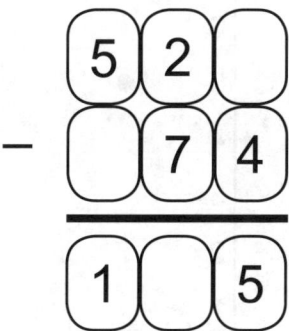

5 2 ☐
− ☐ 7 4
——————
1 ☐ 5

_____
2 marks

7 Look at these numbers.

5.225   5.525   5.22   5.25

Which number is **closest** to 5?

☐

_____
1 mark

What is the **difference** between the largest and smallest numbers in the list?

☐

_____
1 mark

8   Four vertices of a shape have been drawn on this grid.

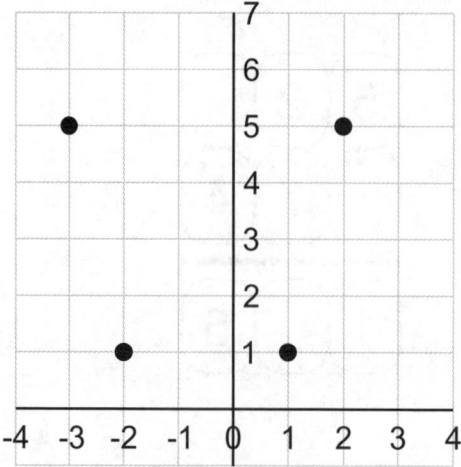

The final vertex of the shape is at **(0, 6)**.

Write the **name** of the shape in the box and circle
regular or **irregular** to make the sentences correct.

The shape is a ⬚ .

It is regular / irregular .

9   What is the largest **odd** factor of 28?

What is the largest multiple of 11 that is **less than** 130?

10 A circus has 17 clowns.

Each clown needs 5 custard pies.

One custard pie uses 35 ml of cream.

How much cream does the circus use in total?

Show your working

| ml |

2 marks

11 Each of these shapes stands for a number.

What number does ⬡ stand for?

Show your working

2 marks

12 Look at the weights of these parcels.

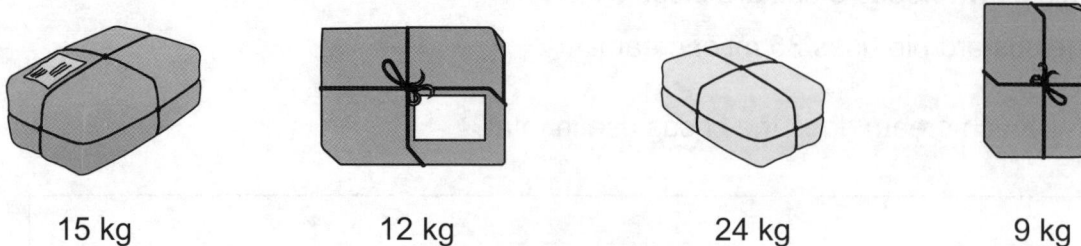

15 kg   12 kg   24 kg   9 kg

What is the mean weight of the four parcels?

| kg |

1 mark

13 Polly is buying some fruit.

5 pineapples cost the same as 8 mangoes.

A mango costs £1.25.

How much does **one** pineapple cost?

Show your working

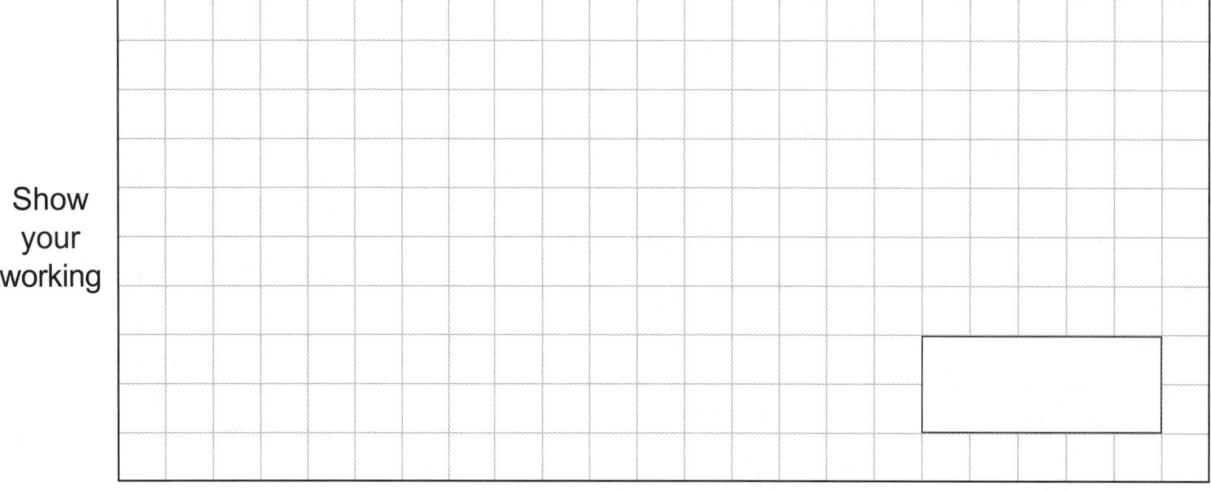

2 marks

14 The diagram shows the design of a flag.

The flag is rectangular, with an area of 96 cm².

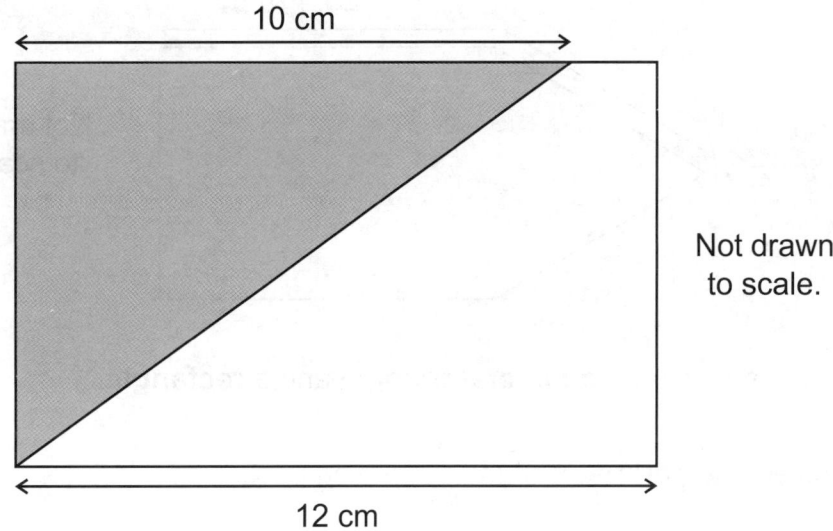

10 cm

Not drawn to scale.

12 cm

What is the area of the grey triangle?

Show your working

cm²

2 marks

15 Complete the calculation to make it correct.

$$2.5 \times \boxed{} = 100$$

1 mark

16 Here is a diagram of a swimming pool.

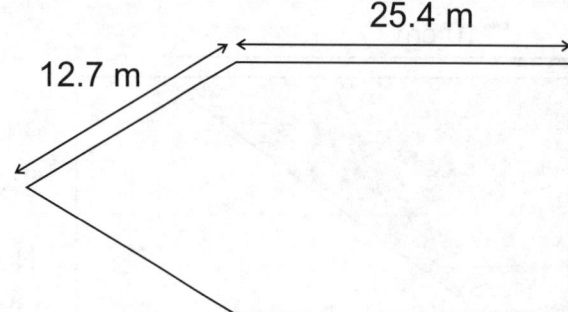

It is made up of an **equilateral triangle** and a **rectangle**.

Calculate the **perimeter** of the swimming pool.

Show your working

	m

2 marks

17 Circle **two** fractions that add together to give $1\frac{3}{7}$.

$\frac{6}{7}$ $\qquad$ $\frac{5}{7}$ $\qquad$ $\frac{11}{7}$ $\qquad$ $\frac{4}{7}$ $\qquad$ $1\frac{1}{7}$ $\qquad$ $1\frac{2}{7}$

1 mark

18   Mina measures these two angles inside a **parallelogram**.

She says "angle A is 130° and angle B is 70°".

Explain how you know that Mina is wrong.
Do **not** use a protractor (angle measurer).

1 mark

19   David is driving in France. He sees a sign that says Paris is 96 km away.

How many **miles** away from Paris is David?

miles

1 mark

20 Aziza is sending books, pens and rubbers in a parcel.

The books weigh 255 g each.

A set of 5 pens weighs 30 g.

Rubbers weigh 20 g each.

Aziza puts 6 books and 20 pens in the parcel.

The total weight of the items in the parcel must be no more than 2 kg.

What is the largest number of rubbers that she can put in the parcel?

Show
your
working

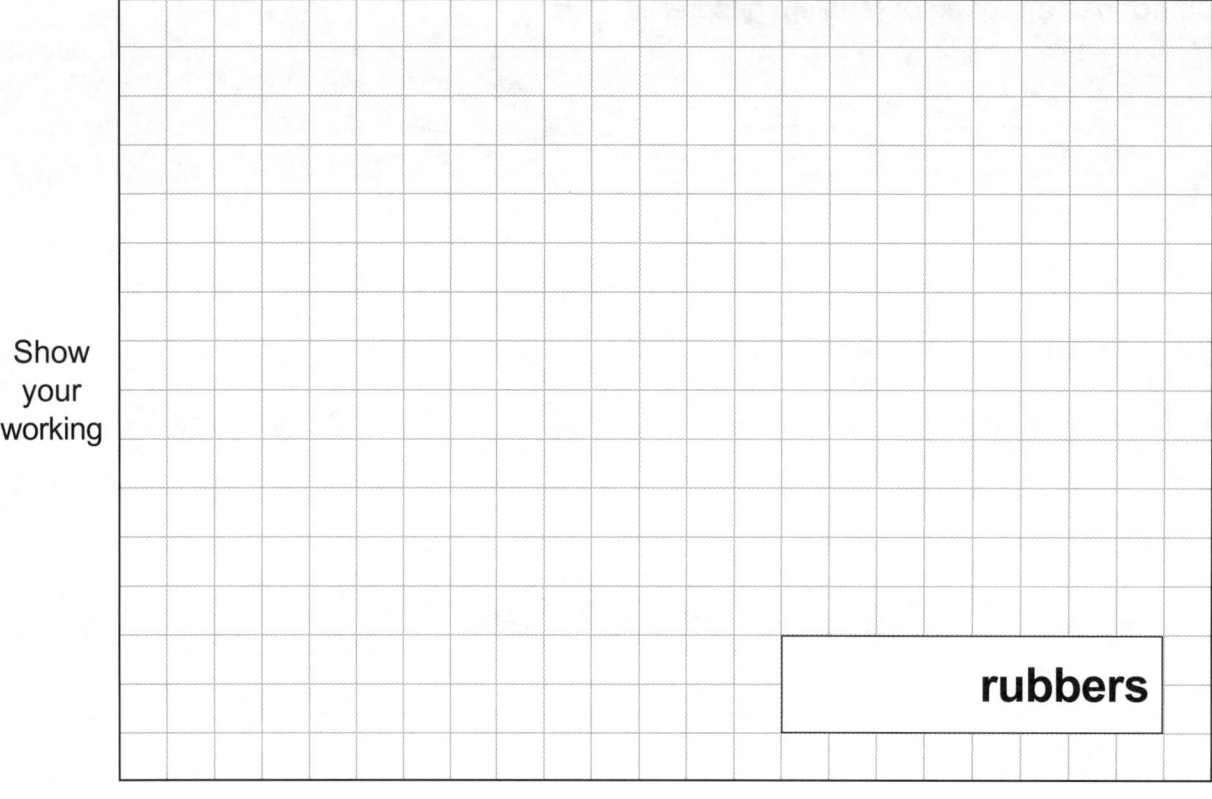

rubbers

3 marks

MHP26U

Key Stage Two Mathematics

Set A
Paper 3: Reasoning

Calculator Not Allowed

40 minutes

First name	
Middle name	
Last name	
School	

Date of birth	Day		Month		Year	

Total marks

Exam Set MHP26

1 The table below shows the number of people at two football stadiums.

	13th August	27th August
Stadium A	9562	7888
Stadium B	8721	8930

How many people **in total** were at the two stadiums on 13th August?

1 mark

How many **fewer** people were at Stadium A on 27th August than on 13th August?

1 mark

2 Circle the number that is made up of **eight tenths** and **three hundredths**.

8.3   0.83   0.38   0.083   0.308

1 mark

3 Complete this net of a square-based pyramid.

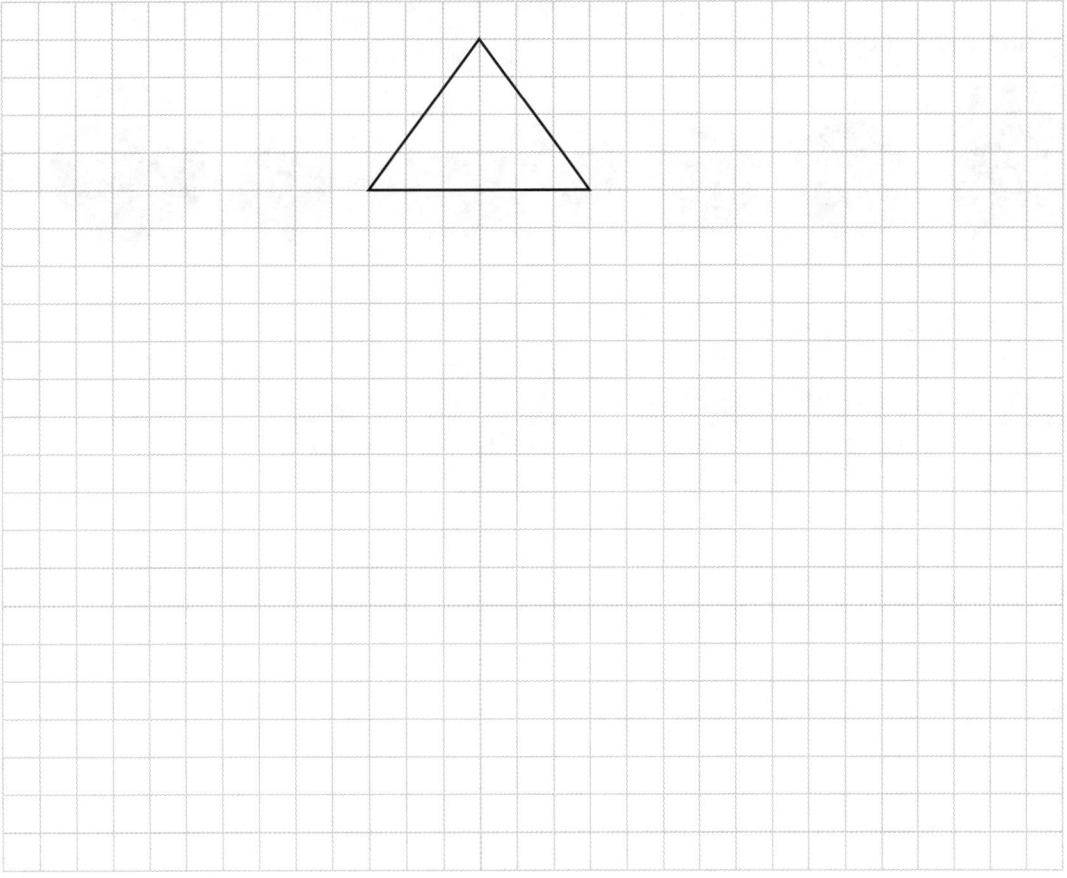

1 mark

4 How many seconds are there in 8 minutes?

seconds

1 mark

How many hours are there in 3 days?

hours

1 mark

5   Tom and Aziza want to put their money together to buy a kite.

Tom has these coins.

Aziza has these coins.

The kite costs £10.

How much more money do they need?

Show your working

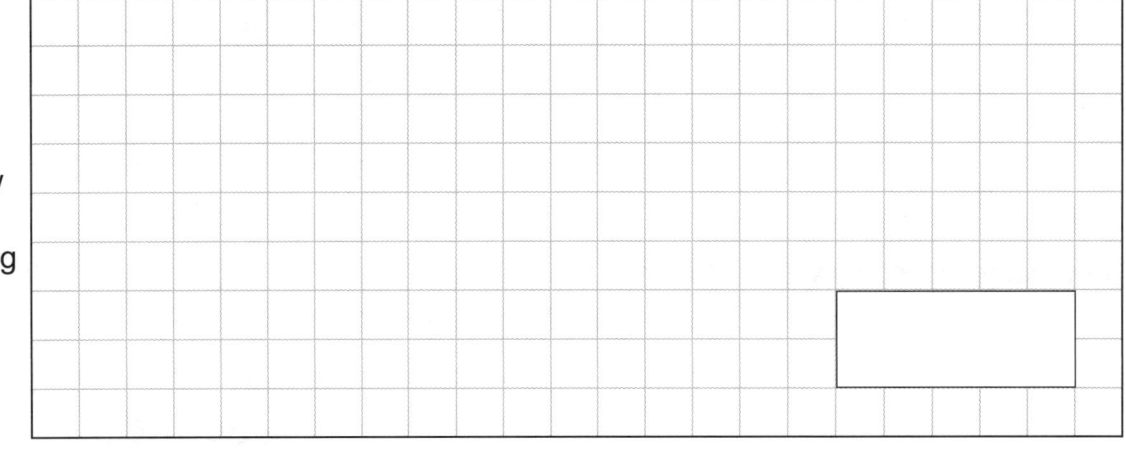

_____
2 marks

6   Fill in the next two numbers in this sequence.

27   46   65   ☐   ☐

_____
1 mark

7 Draw lines to match each angle with the word that describes it.

Reflex	Acute	Obtuse

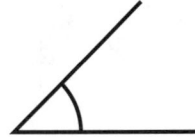  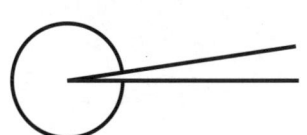

2 marks

8 Part of a bus timetable is shown below.

Diamond Street	13:23	13:55	14:05	14:23
Rhombus Road	13:31	14:03	14:13	14:31
Kite Square	13:36	14:08	14:18	14:36
Trapezium Alley	13:42	14:14	14:24	14:42

How long does the bus take to get from Diamond Street to Trapezium Alley?

minutes

1 mark

Tom catches a bus from Diamond Street. It leaves on time.
At quarter past two the bus is **between** Rhombus Road and Kite Square.

What time did the bus leave Diamond Street?

1 mark

9   A number has **three** prime factors.
Two of its prime factors are 3 and 5.
The other prime factor is even.

Put a tick in the outline that shows the

What is the number?

10   The grey shape is translated **3 squares up** and **6 squares to the right**.

Put a tick in the outline that shows the
position of the shape after this translation.

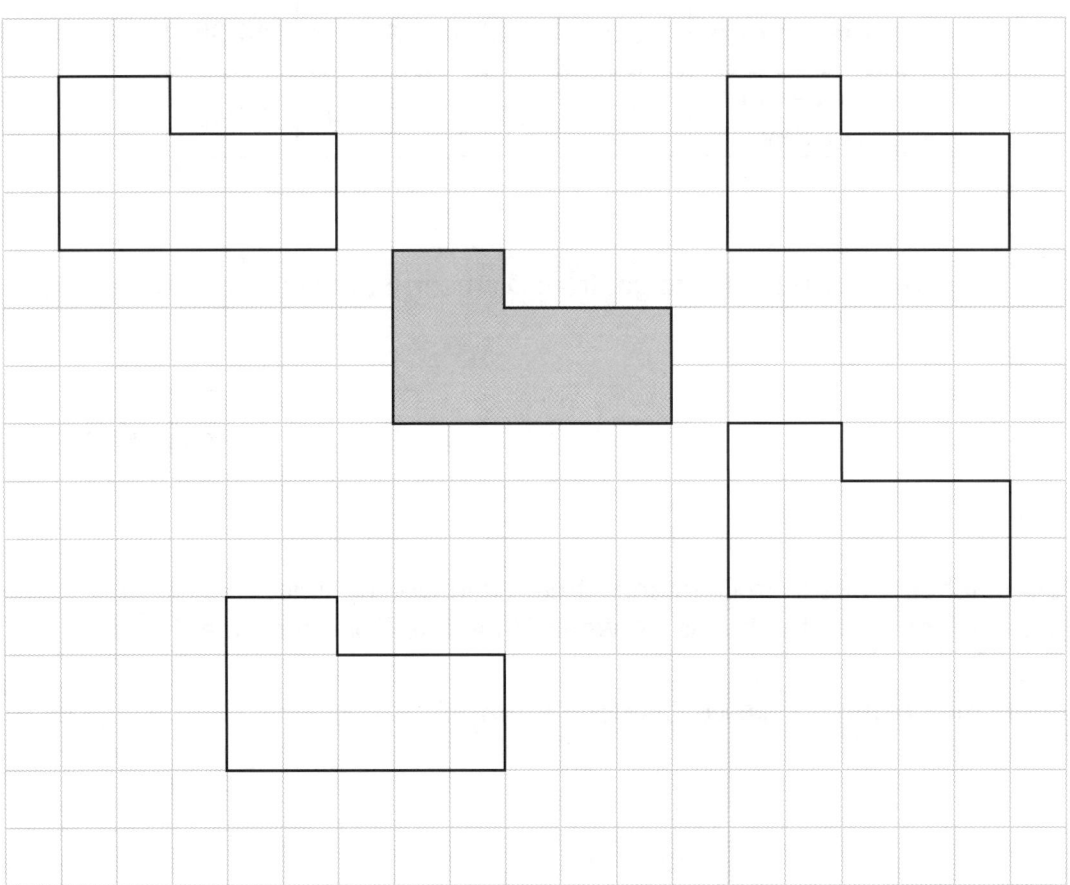

11   a = 2b

b = 44

What is the value of a?

_____
1 mark

5c + 50 = 75

What is the value of c?

_____
1 mark

12   Aziza mixes different colours to make green paint.

$\dfrac{2}{5}$ of the paint she uses is blue.

The green paint she makes fills **four 250 ml pots**.

How much **blue** paint does she use in total?

Show your working

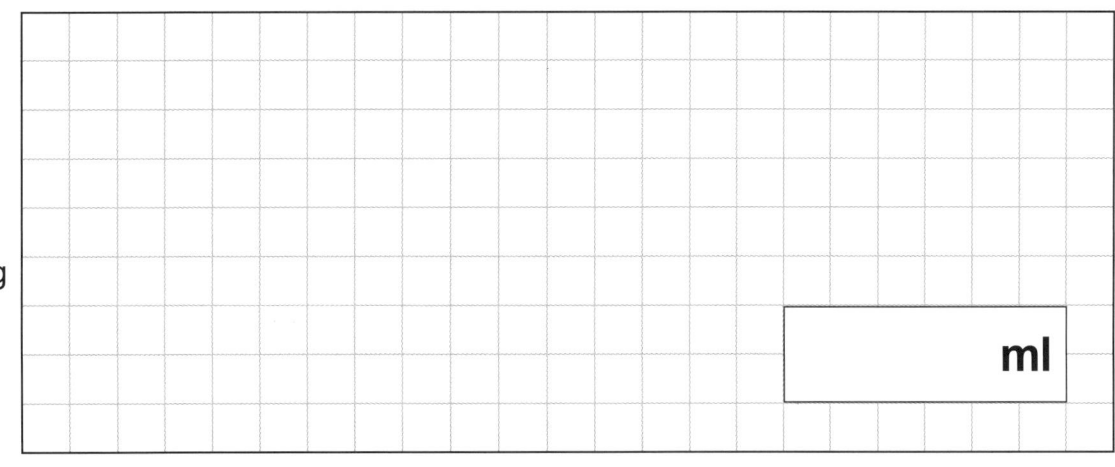

ml

_____
2 marks

Here is a calculation.

$$5.8 \times 49\ 998$$

Fill in the boxes to show how you could **estimate** the answer to this calculation.

	×		=	

Is your estimate **more** or **less** than the actual answer?
Explain how you know.

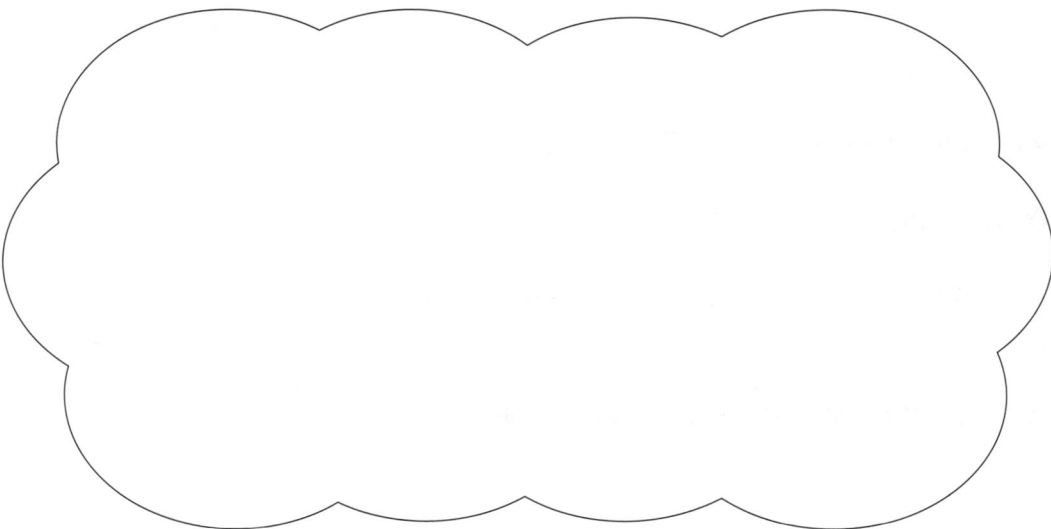

14 Look at these Roman numerals.

XC   XXV   LXIV

Write each Roman numeral in the correct place on the diagram.

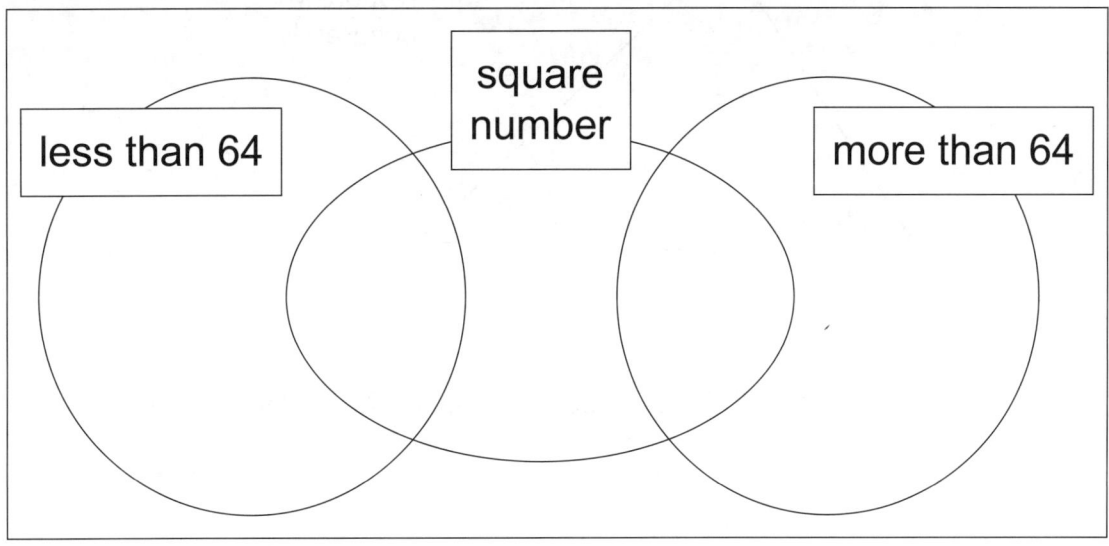

2 marks

15 Tom's desk is 0.7 m tall.

His desk is half as tall as his drawers.

His drawers are 0.5 m shorter than his wardrobe.

How tall is Tom's wardrobe?

Show your working

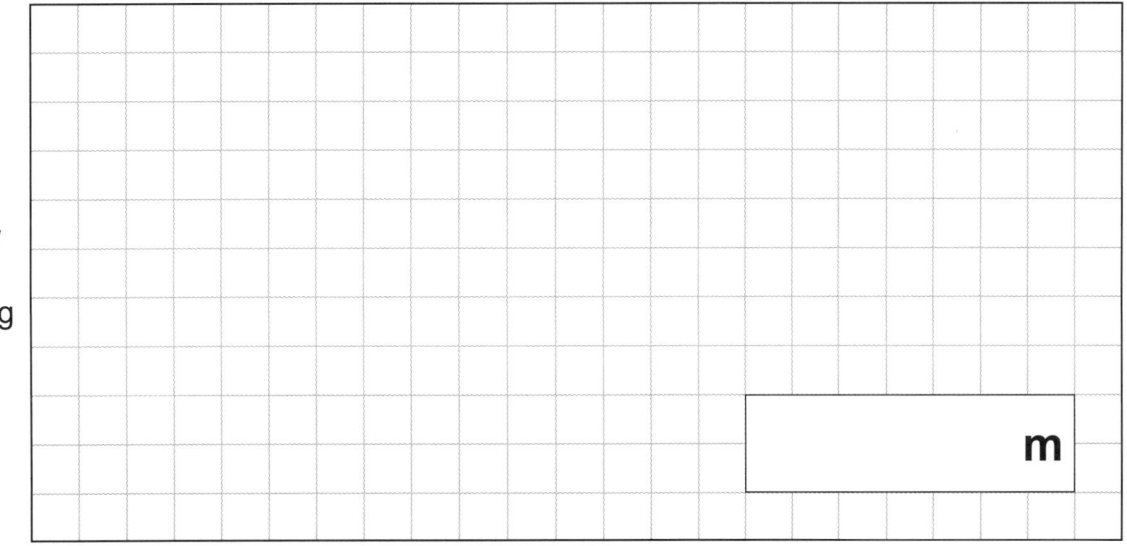

m

2 marks

16   Look at this diagram.

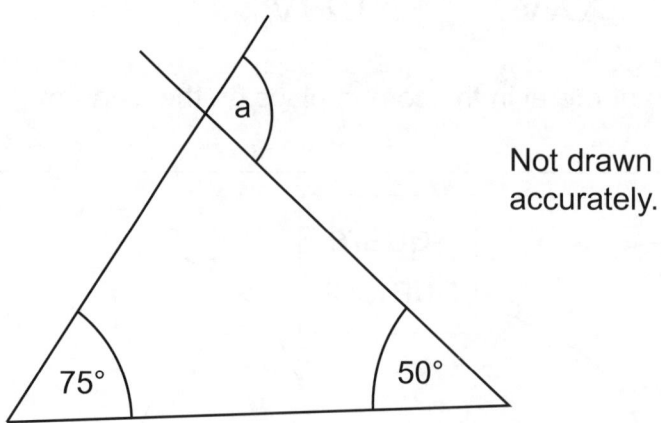

Not drawn
accurately.

75°   50°

What is the size of angle a?   Do not use a protractor (angle measurer).

Show
your
working

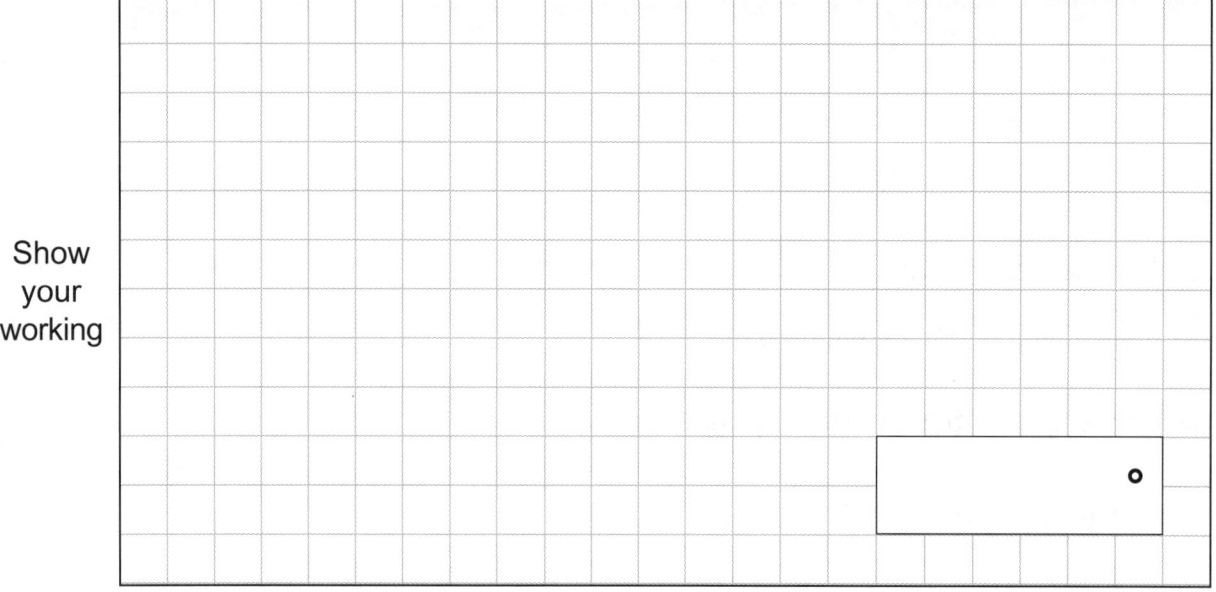

°

2 marks

17　A dessert recipe needs 25 ml of syrup for every 80 g of ice cream used.

One day, a restaurant uses 4 kg of ice cream to make the desserts.

How many **litres** of syrup do they use?

Show
your
working

| litres |

18　Fill in the boxes to make these calculations correct.

$$\frac{5}{6} \div \boxed{} = \frac{5}{18}$$

$$\frac{2}{3} \boxed{} \frac{6}{7} = \frac{4}{7}$$

19 Kishan is doing a sponsored swim.

He has done $\frac{5}{7}$ of the swim.

He still has another 100 m to go.

How long is the sponsored swim?

Show your working

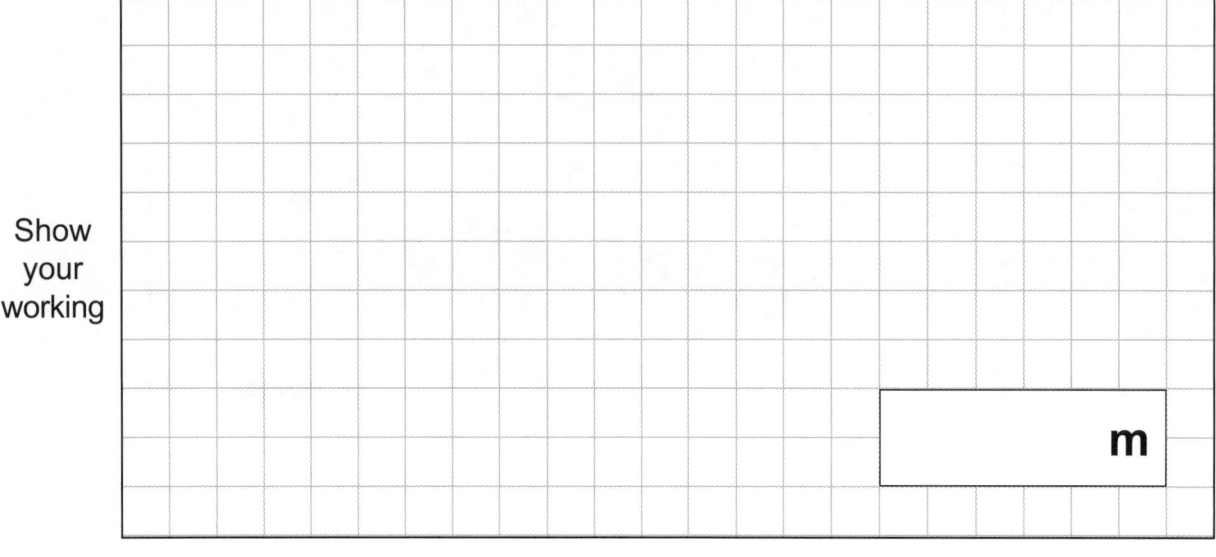

	m

2 marks

20 Add brackets to make each calculation correct.

$$5 \times 7 - 3 + 4 = 24$$

1 mark

$$6 - 3 \times 4 + 8 = 36$$

1 mark

Key Stage Two Mathematics

Set B
Paper 1: Arithmetic

Calculator Not Allowed

30 minutes

First name	
Middle name	
Last name	
School	

Date of birth	Day		Month		Year	

Total marks

1   50 × 3 =

2   [   ] = 7 ÷ 7

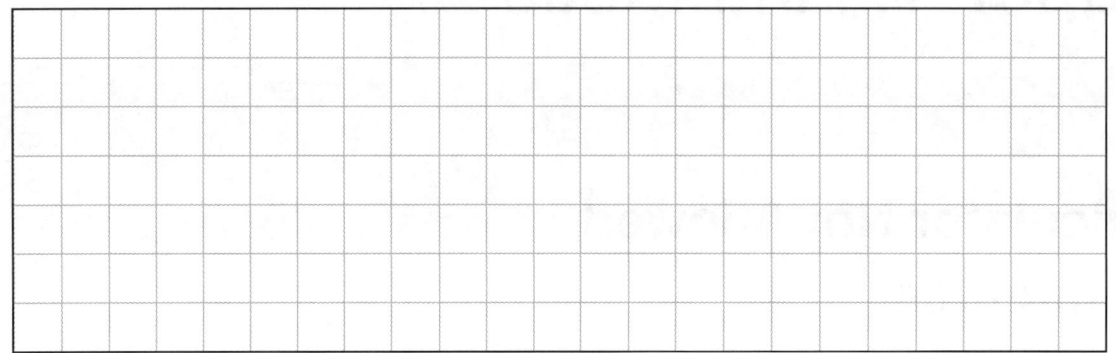

3   55 + 2050 =

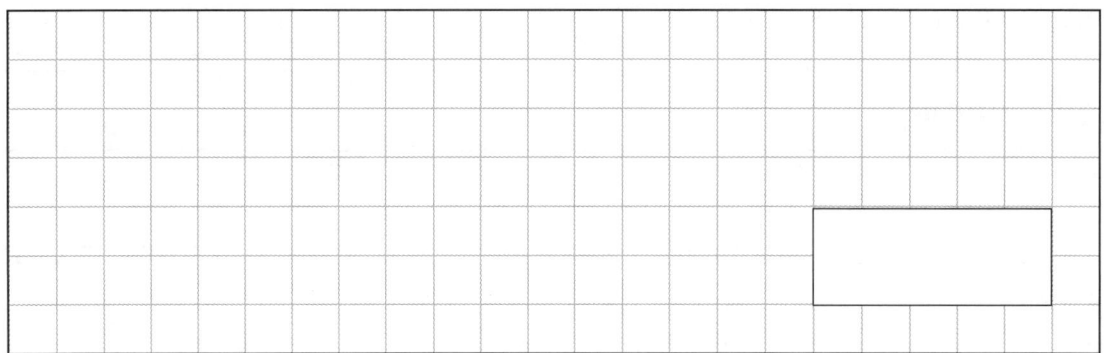

4   462 − 41 =

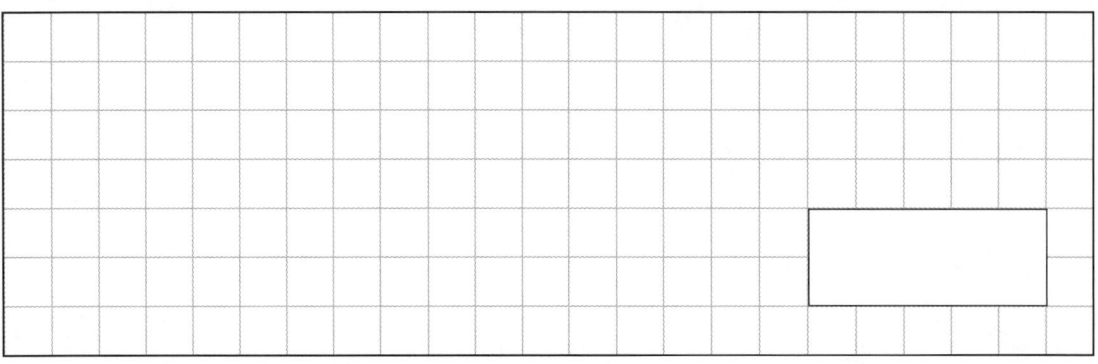

5 $11 \times 8 =$

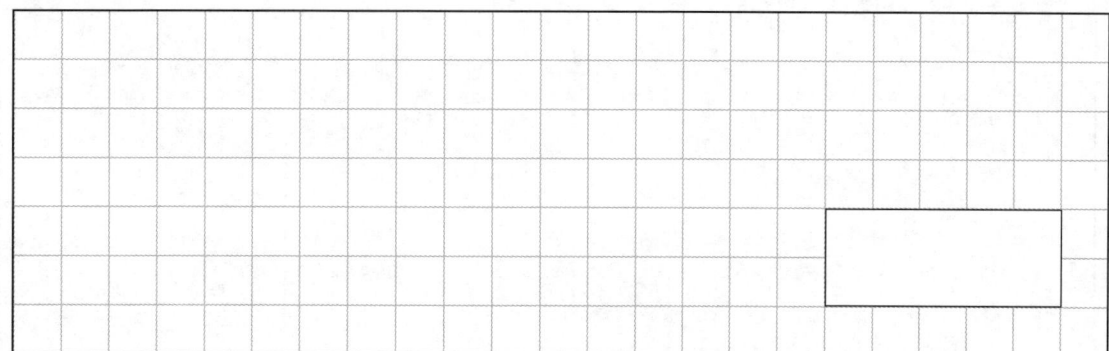

6 $0.4 + 1.6 =$

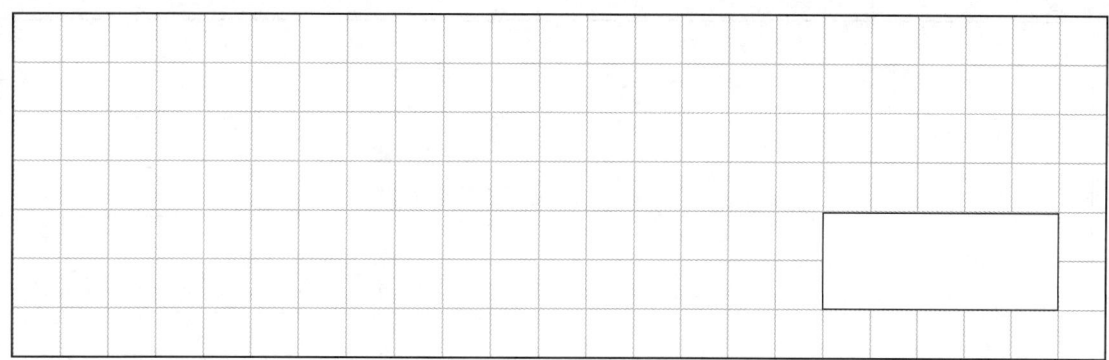

7 $96 \div 8 =$

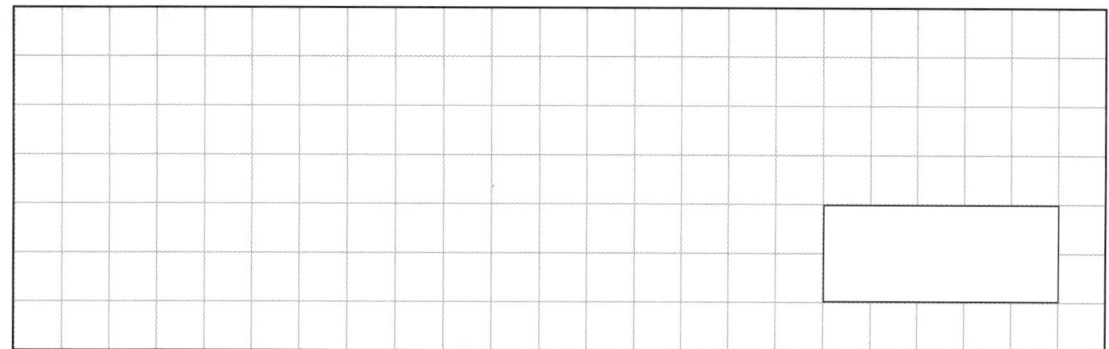

8 $70\ 006 + 7995 =$

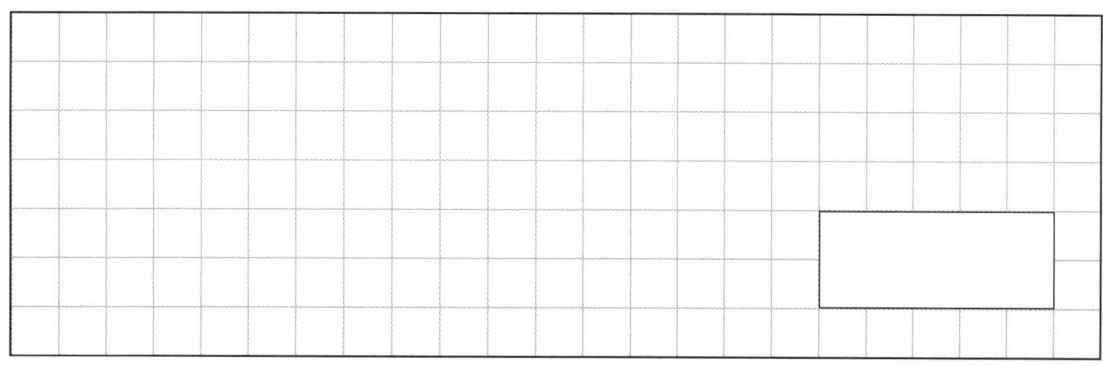

9 $80 \times 70 =$

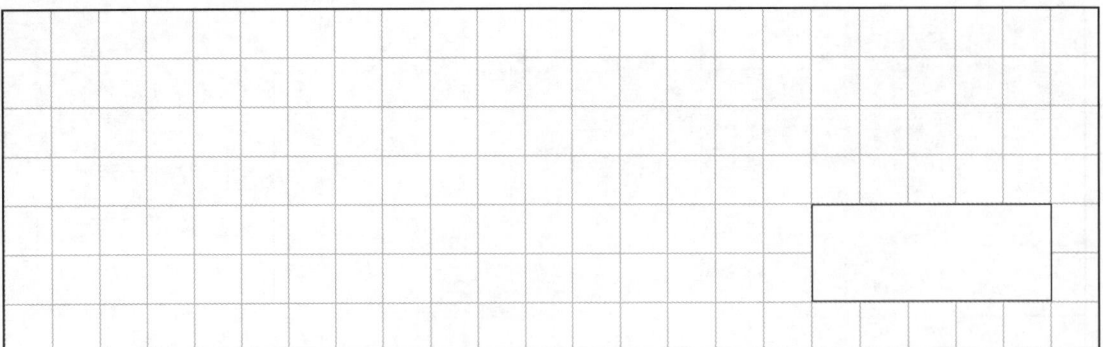

1 mark

10 $30\ 000 - 800 =$

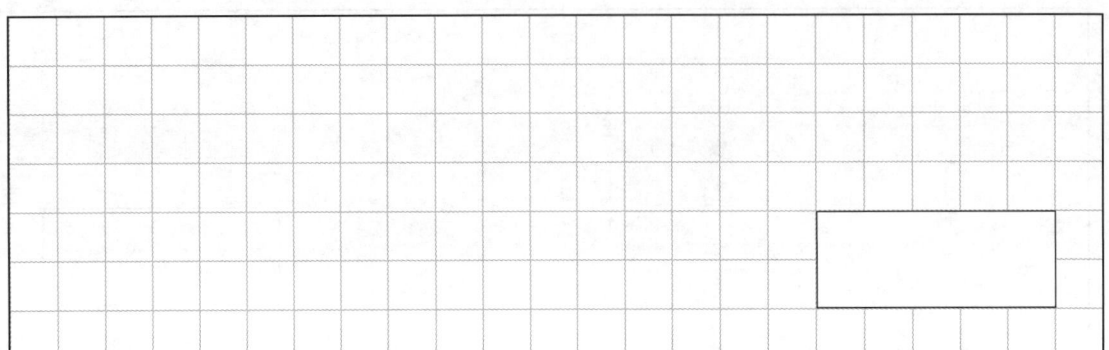

1 mark

11 $746 \times 5 =$

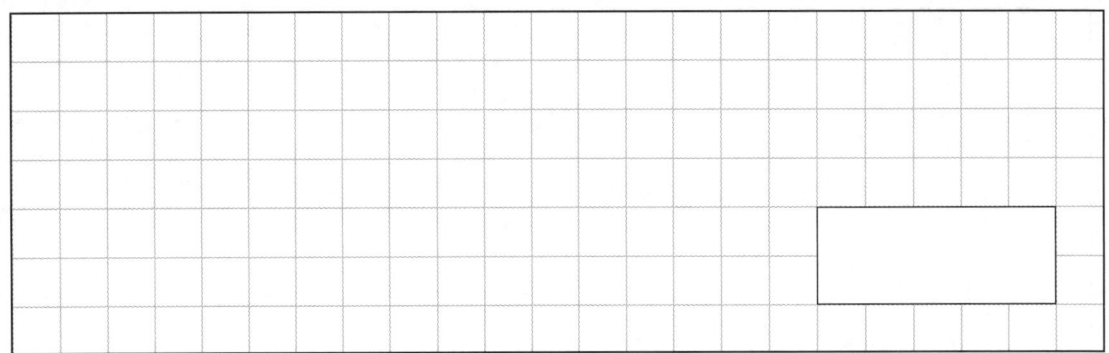

1 mark

12 $89 \times 1000 =$

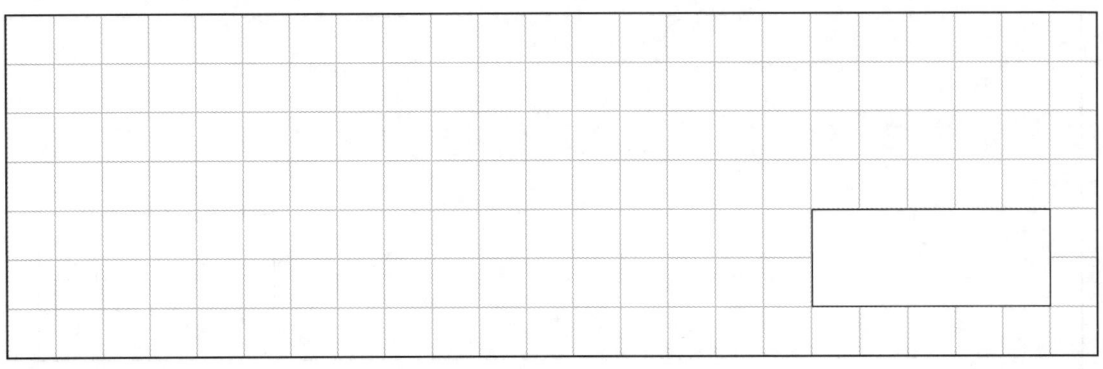

1 mark

13 582 ÷ 6 =

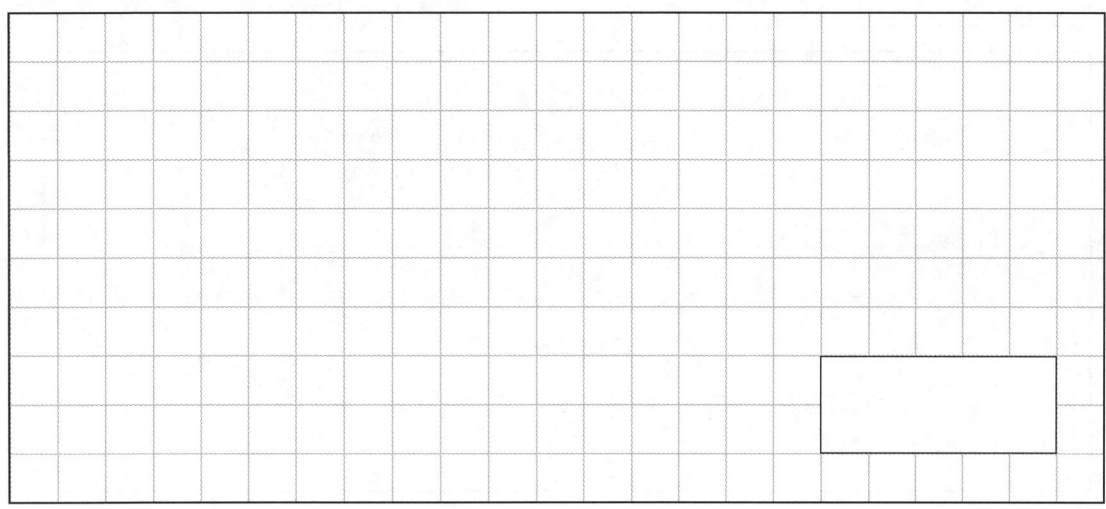

1 mark

14 20.002 + 1.18 =

1 mark

15 36 ÷ 100 =

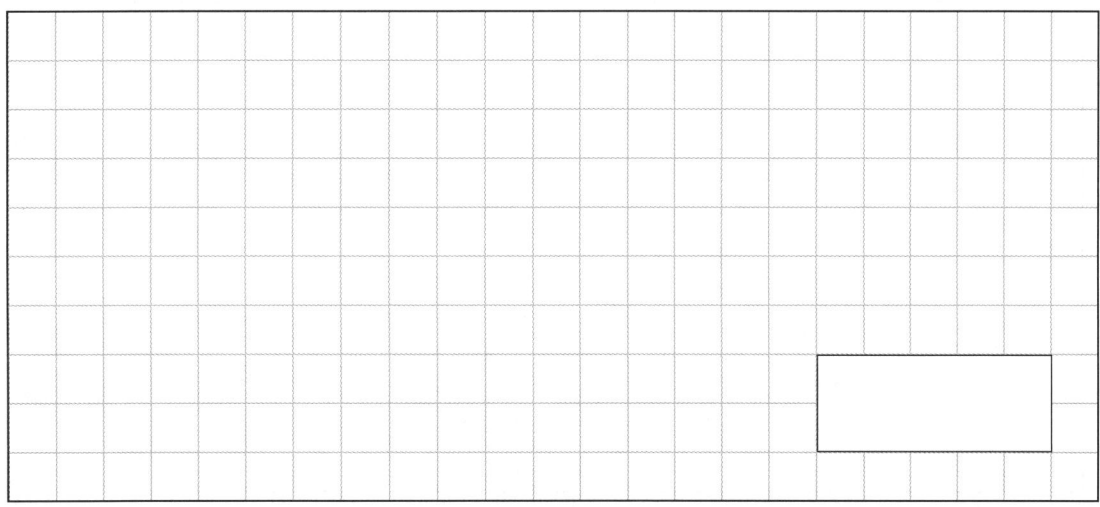

1 mark

16 ☐ = 30 216 − 5492

17 10% of 640 =

18 333.36 − 21.21 =

19

$$\frac{11}{13} - \frac{5}{13} =$$

1 mark

20

$5^2 + 5 =$

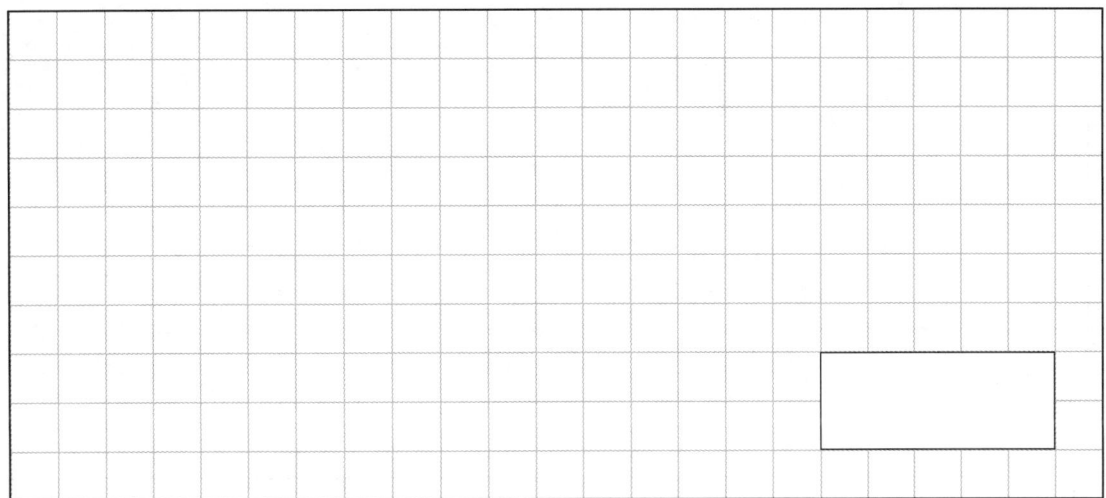

1 mark

21

$680\ 501 - 12\ 689 =$

1 mark

22 $8400 \div 12 =$

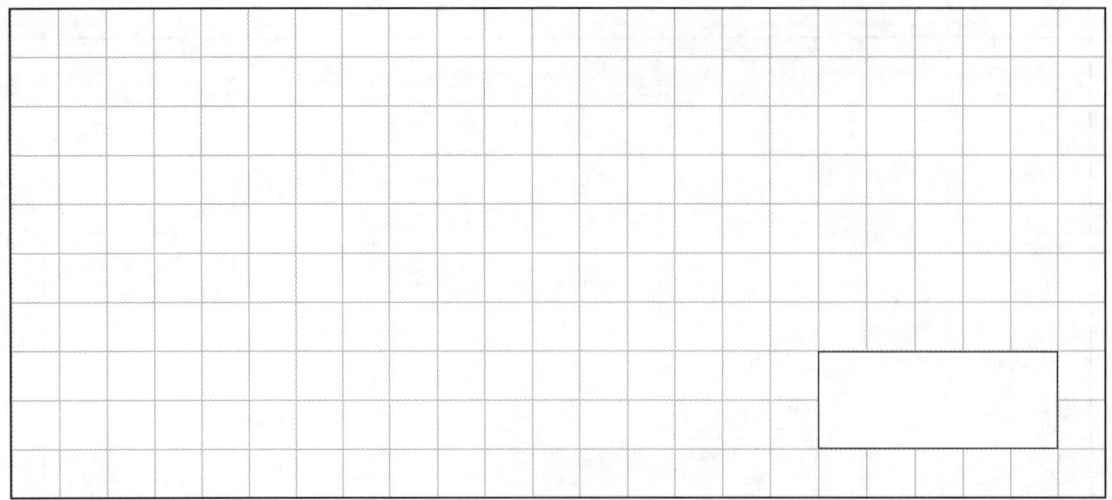

1 mark

23 $8 - 4.35 =$

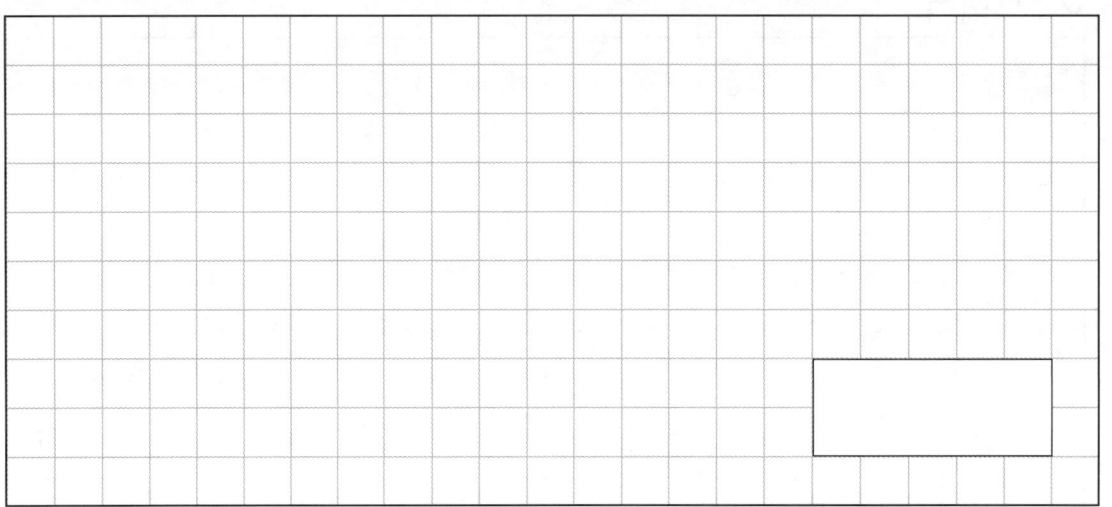

1 mark

24

Show your working

$$\begin{array}{r} 5\ 9 \\ \times\ \ 5\ 2 \\ \hline \end{array}$$

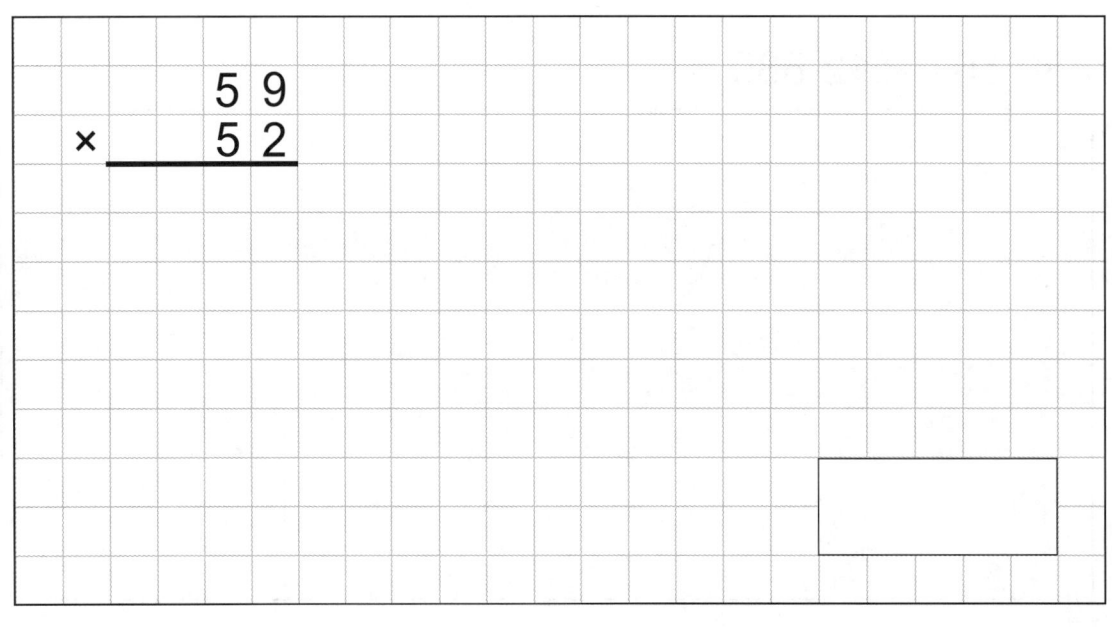

2 marks

25 $1\dfrac{2}{3} + \dfrac{2}{3} =$

26 $\dfrac{1}{6} \times \dfrac{1}{7} =$

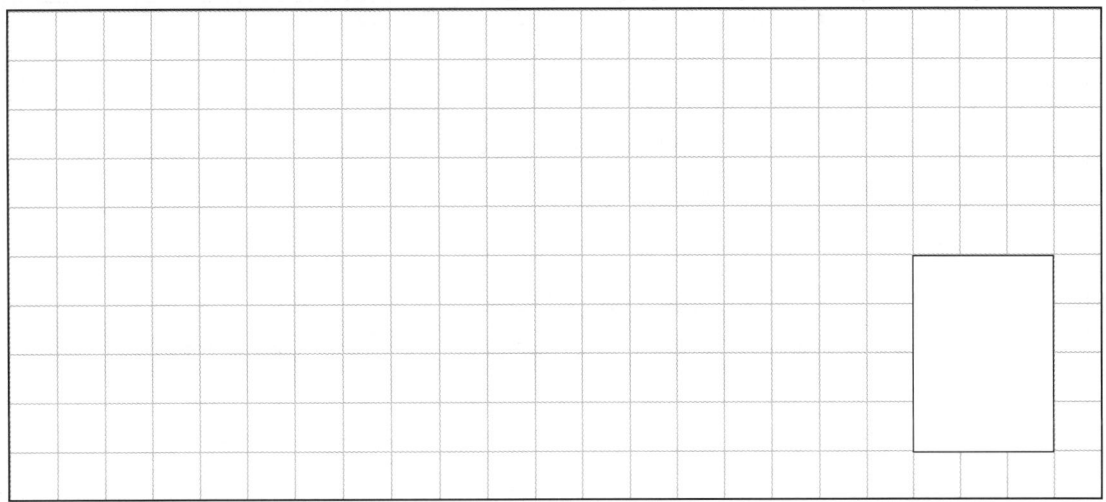

27

Show your working

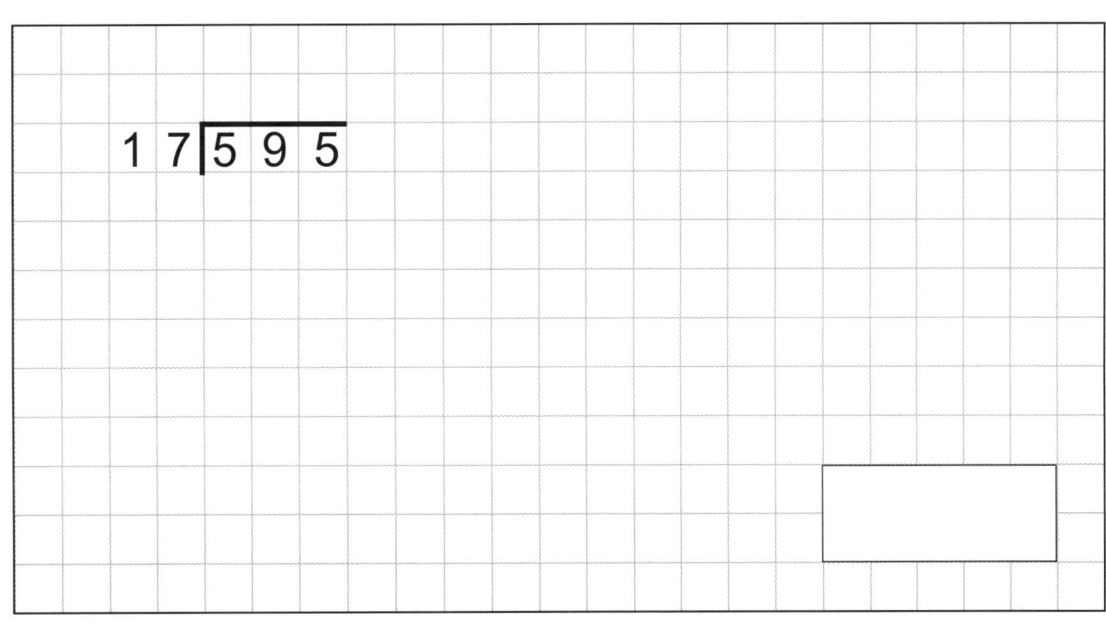

$17\overline{)595}$

---

28 $15 \times \dfrac{3}{5} =$

1 mark

29 $13 \times 5.6 =$

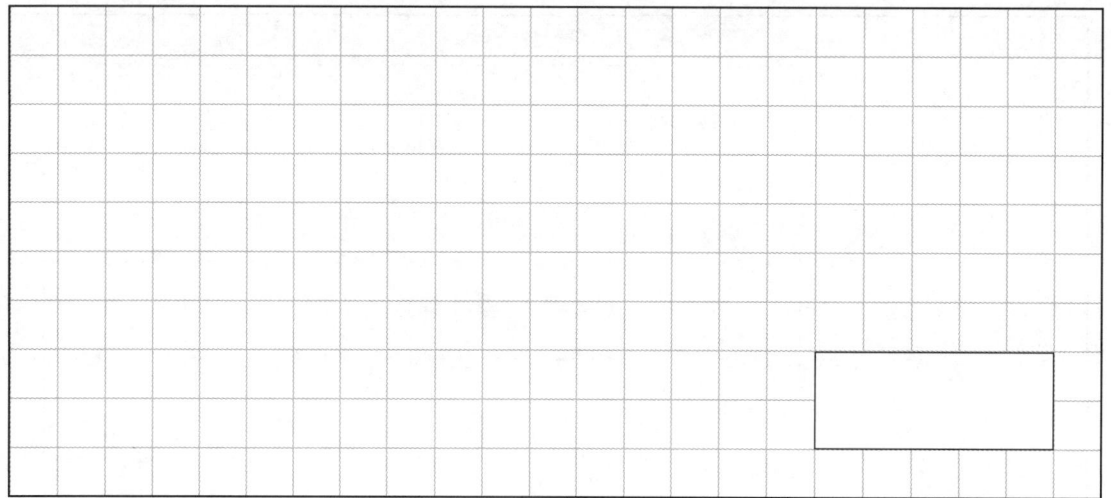

1 mark

30 $85\% \times 80 =$

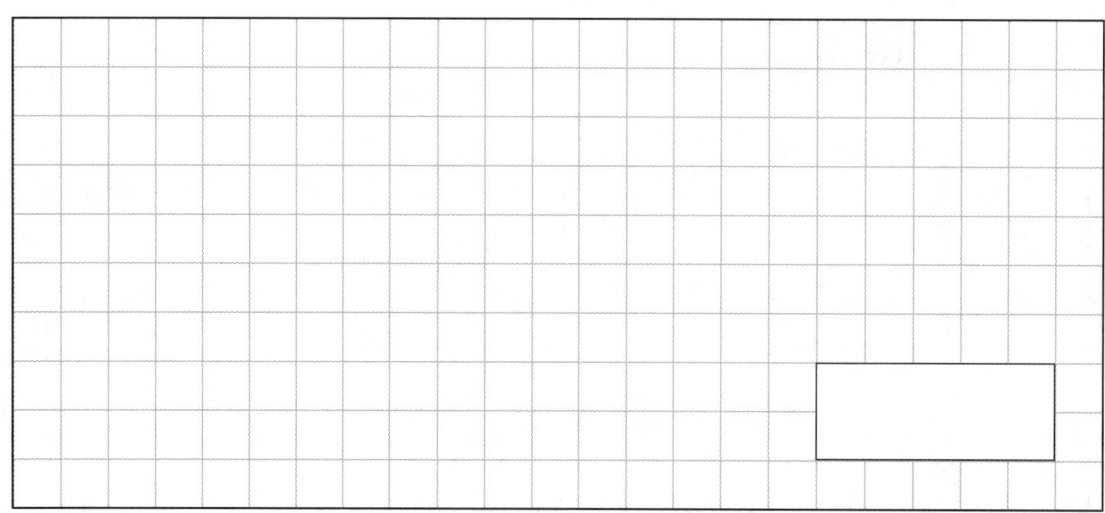

1 mark

31

$$\frac{13}{14} + \frac{1}{28} =$$

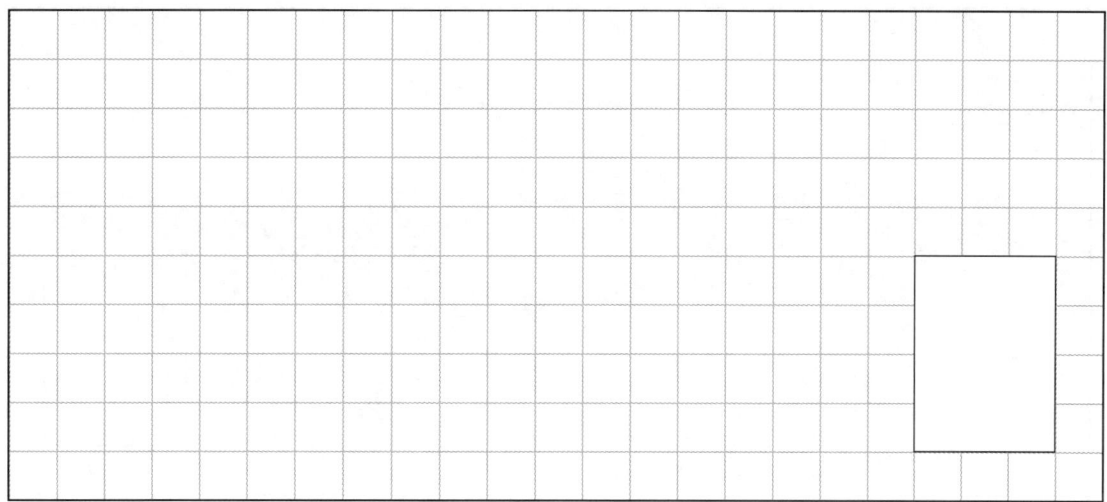

1 mark

32

$$
\begin{array}{r}
3\ 7\ 8\ 4 \\
\times \qquad 2\ 6 \\
\hline
\end{array}
$$

Show your working

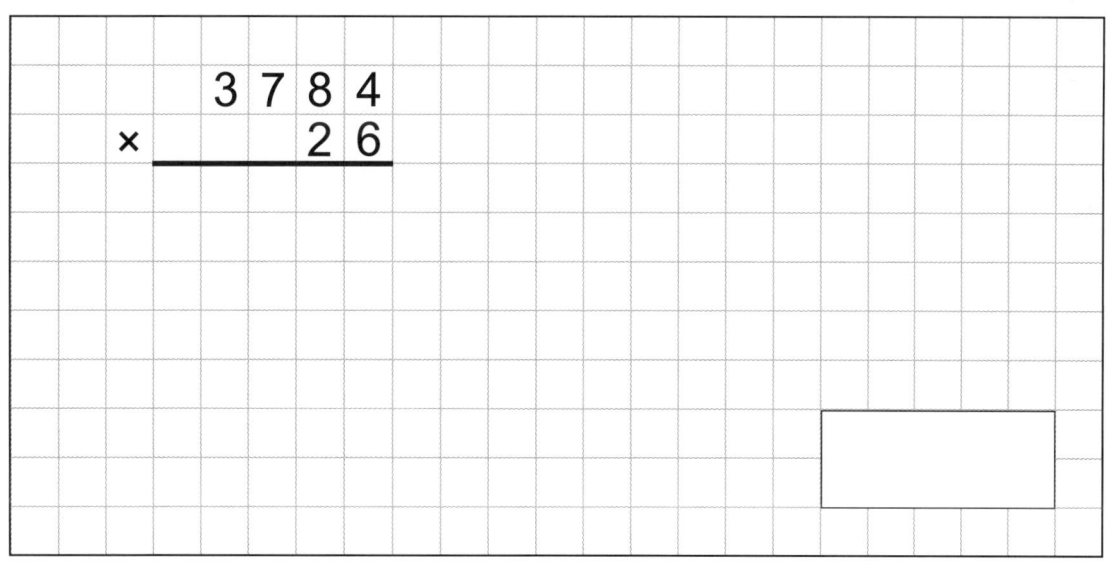

2 marks

33

$$3\ 7\,\overline{)\,2\ 7\ 0\ 1}$$

Show your working

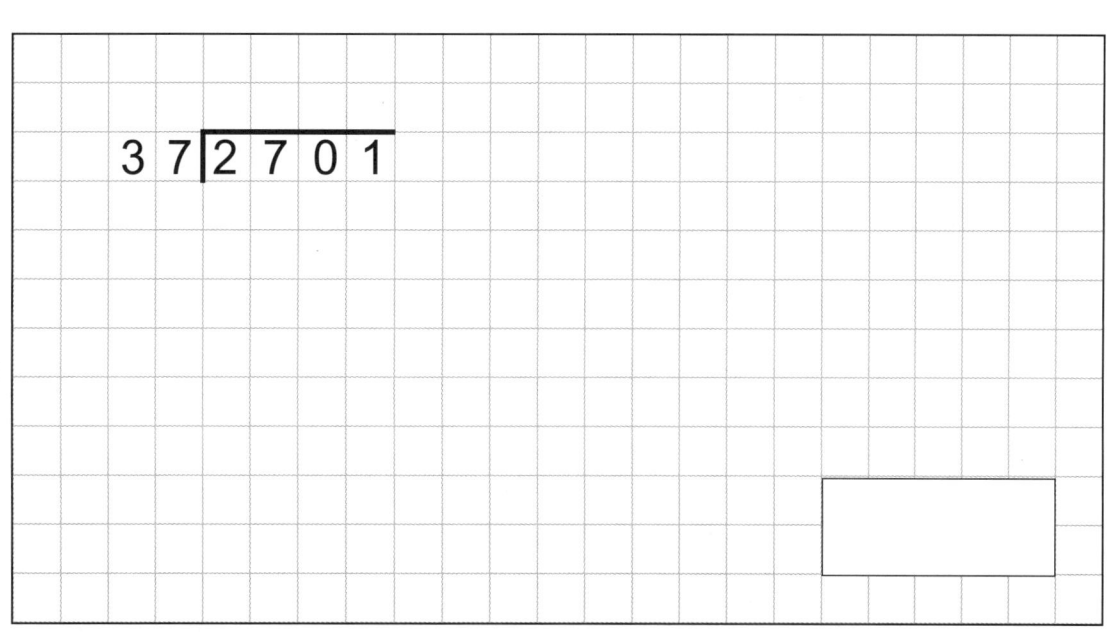

2 marks

34 $1\dfrac{2}{3} - \dfrac{3}{4} =$

35 $\dfrac{4}{5} \div 5 =$

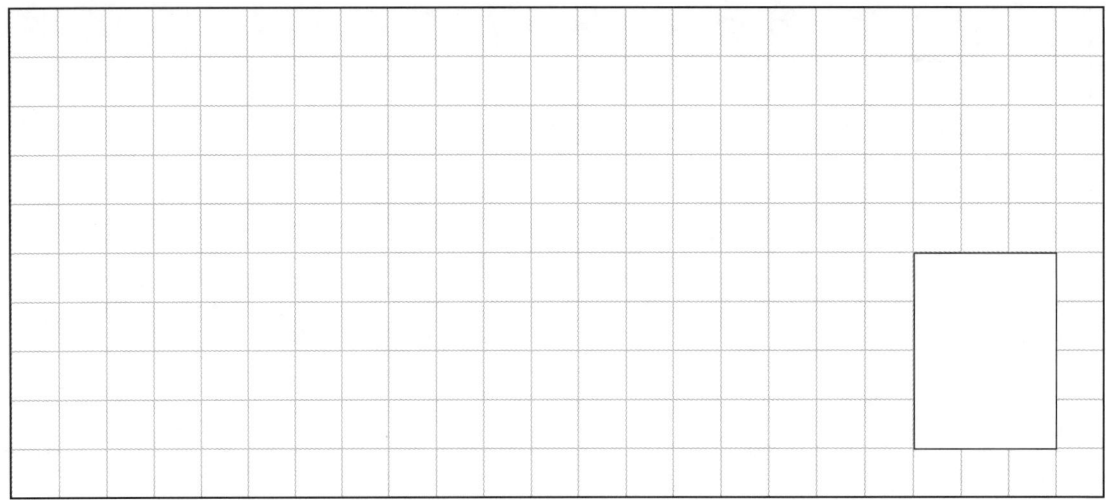

36 $(10 - 2) + 14 \times 2 =$

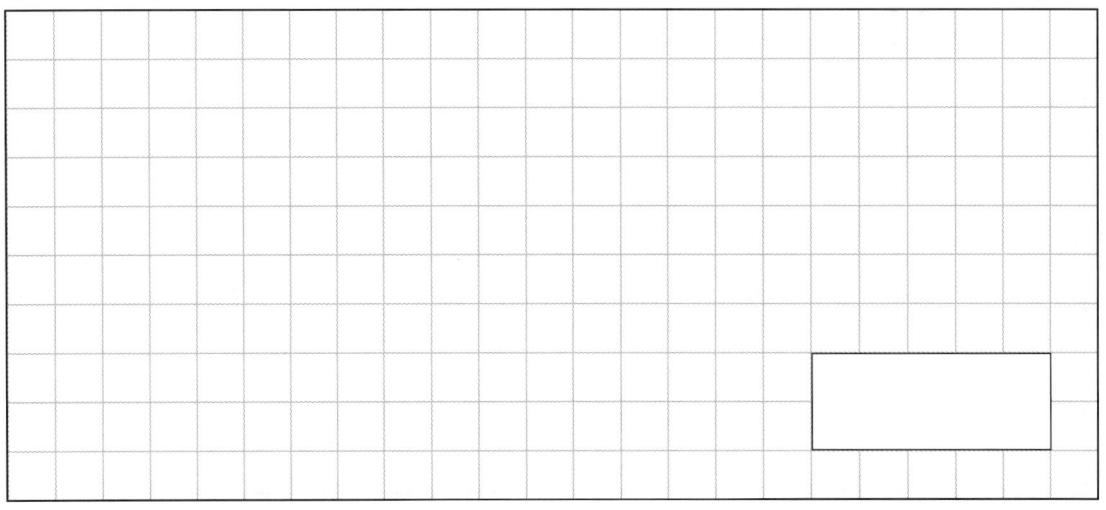

© CGP 2020 — copying more than
5% of this paper is not permitted

MHP26U

Key Stage Two Mathematics

Set B
Paper 2: Reasoning

Calculator Not Allowed

40 minutes

First name	
Middle name	
Last name	
School	

Date of birth	Day		Month		Year	

Total marks

1 Complete this number sequence.

45 294   35 294   25 294   

1 mark

2 The bar chart shows the shoe sizes of some children in a youth club.

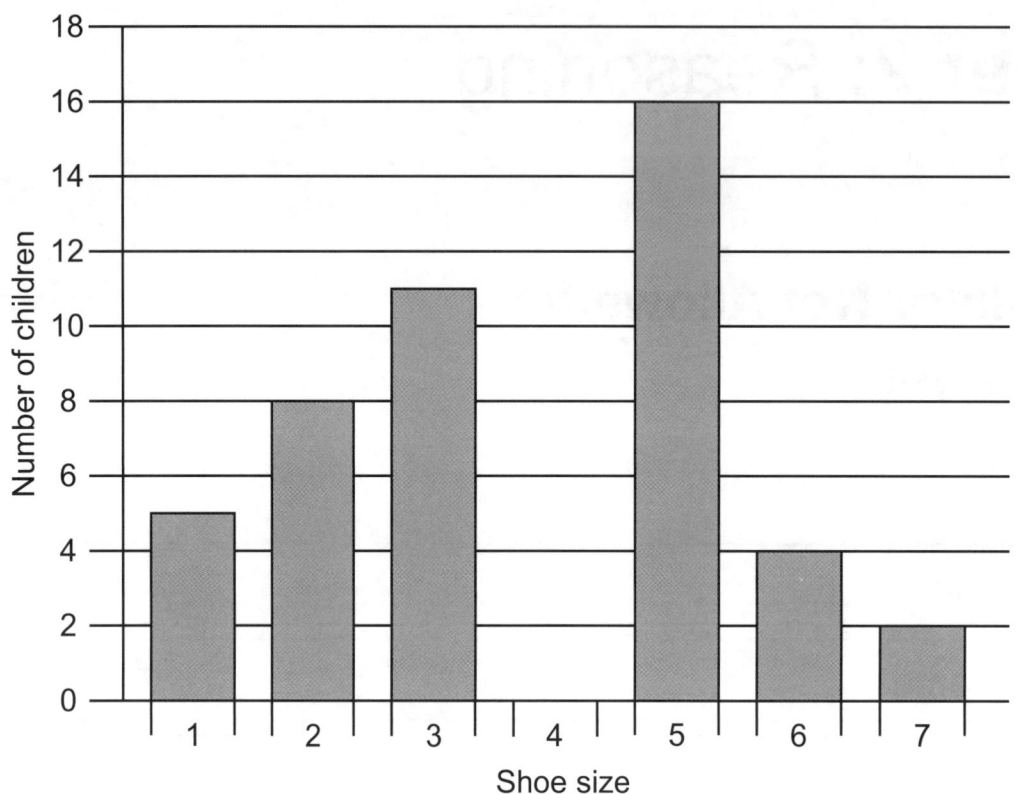

Shoe size

The number of children with size 4 feet was **half** the number of children with size 5 feet.

Draw a bar on the bar chart to show this.

1 mark

How many children have a shoe size of **3 or smaller**?

children

1 mark

3 Write down two **prime** numbers that add together to give 24.

[　　　　] and [　　　　]

1 mark

4 A garage sells these two cars in one day.

£31 765   £18 999

How much money does the garage make **in total**?

[　　　　　　　]

1 mark

What is the **difference** between the price of the two cars?

[　　　　　　　]

1 mark

5 Put these numbers in order from smallest to largest.

0.82   0.783   1.02   0.824   1.1

smallest   largest

1 mark

6 The diagrams show the displays on two clocks at the same time one afternoon.

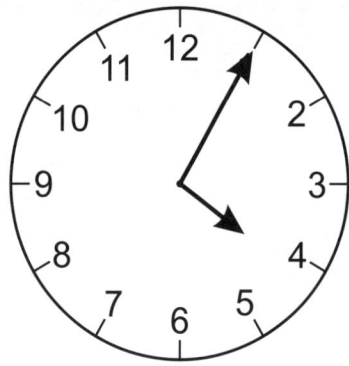

This clock shows
the correct time.

15:57

This clock is slow.

How many minutes **slow** is the digital clock?

minutes

1 mark

7 Draw **two** rectangles on the grid below.
Both rectangles must have an **area of 6 square units**.
They must have **different perimeters**.

8 Four trumpets are **192 cm** long in total.

Two trumpets and a clarinet are **155 cm** long in total.

How long is the **clarinet**?

Show your working

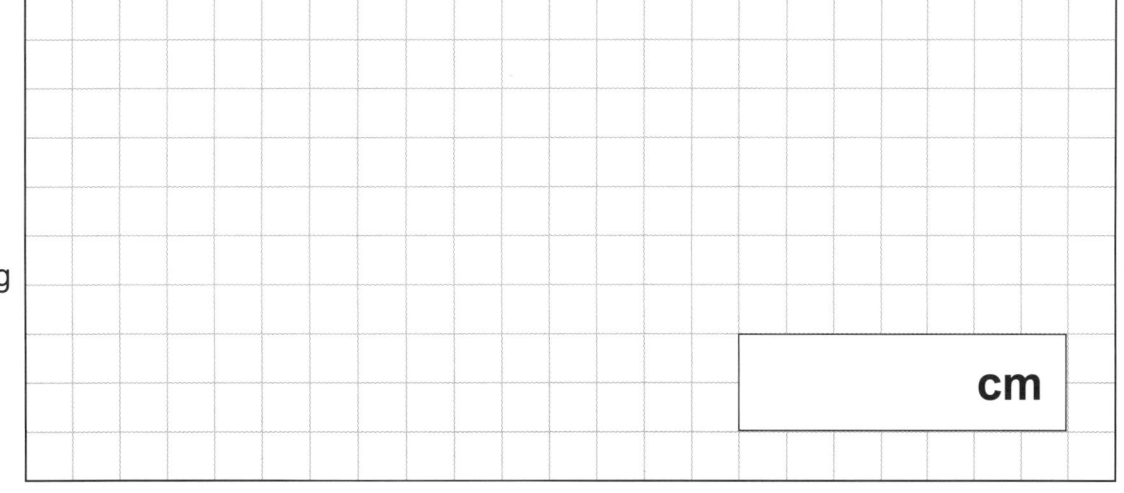

cm

         KS2 Maths / Set B / Paper 2

9 Juan walks the same distance each day for seven days.
He walks 6.3 km in total.

How many **metres** does he walk each day?

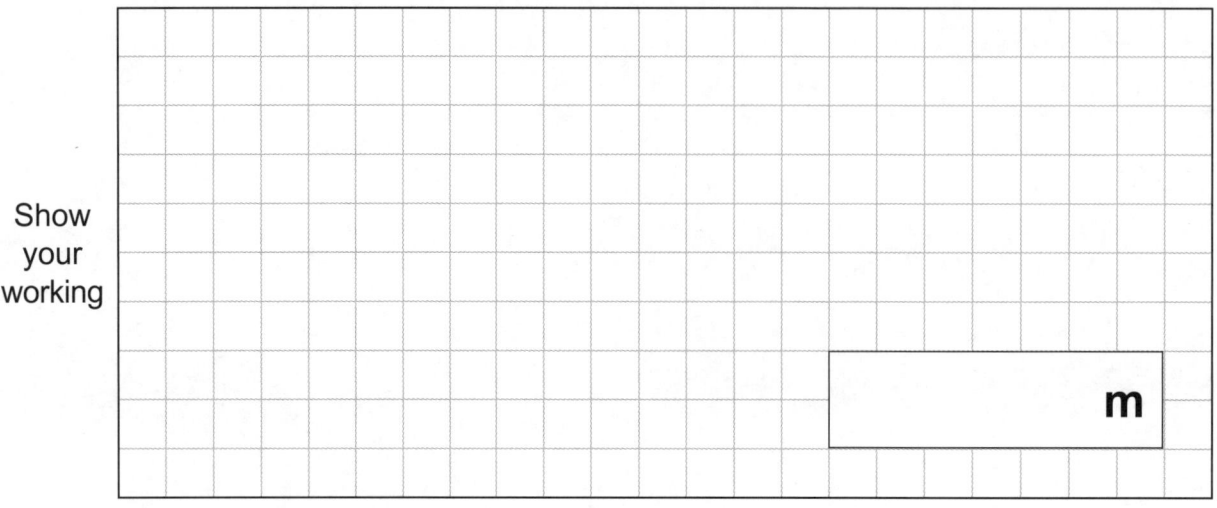

Show
your
working

m

2 marks

10 Shade $\frac{2}{3}$ of each of these shapes.

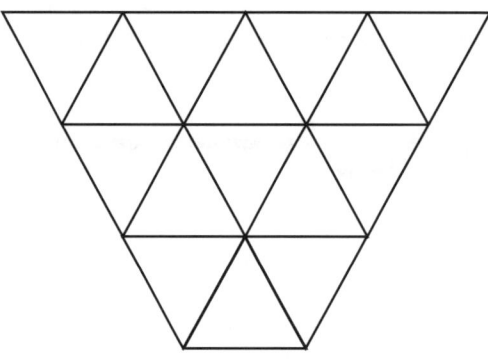

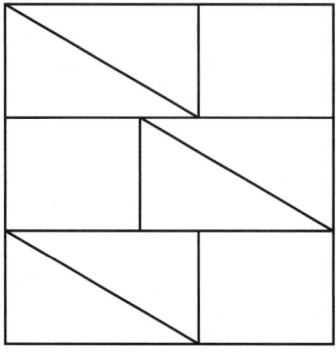

2 marks

11   The cost of hiring a hall for a party can be worked out using this formula.

$$\text{Cost} = £5.50 \times \text{number of people} + £50$$

> How much would it cost to hire the hall for **20** people?

1 mark

12   Fill in the box to make this calculation correct.

$$\frac{2}{5} + \frac{\square}{10} = 1\frac{1}{10}$$

1 mark

13   Circle two numbers that add together to give **2**.

1.48   0.502   1.598   0.42   0.402

1 mark

14 Polly measures the temperature in her bedroom, garden and garage one evening in January.

Bedroom   Garden

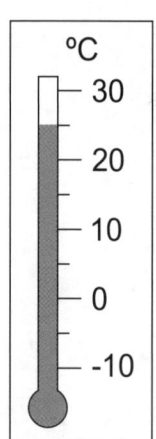   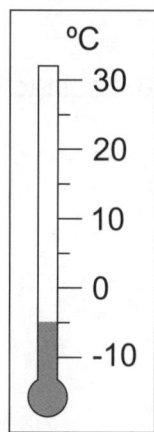

The temperature in the garage is **halfway** between these two temperatures.

What temperature is the garage?

Show
your
working

°C

2 marks

15 Write one number in each box of the table below.
One has been done for you.

	Multiple of 8	Number ending in 2
Multiple of 6		
Number starting with 3		302

2 marks

16 Two points have been marked on the grid below.

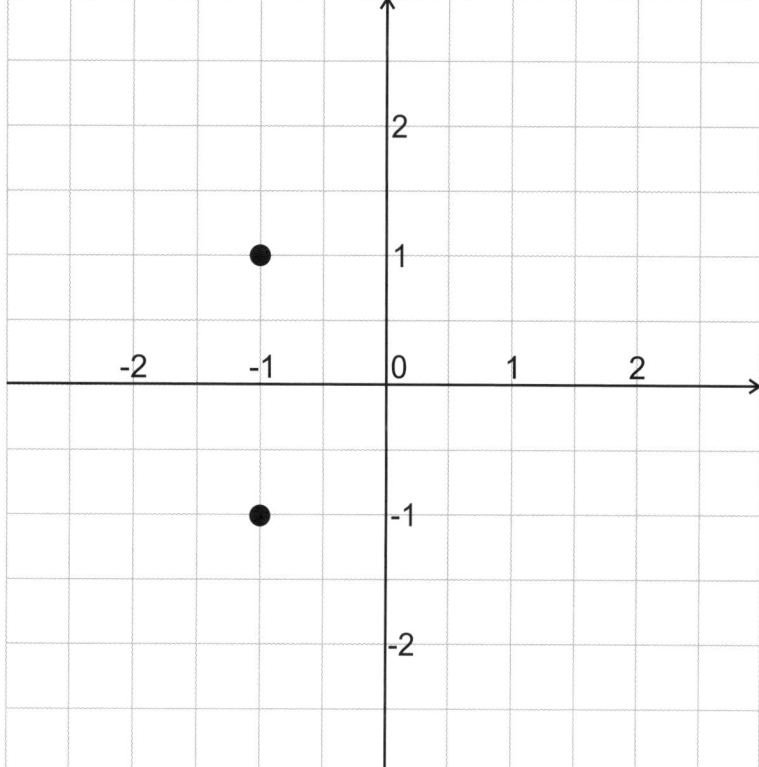

Lizzy adds another point to the grid and joins
the points to make an **isosceles** triangle.

Circle **all** the coordinates that could be the point she added.

(0, 0)   (-2, 1)   (1, -1)   (0, 2)   (2, 0)   (-1, 2)

2 marks

17 3 large buckets hold the **same** amount of water as 5 small buckets.

It takes **12** large buckets of water to fill a **60 litre** tub.

How much water does one small bucket hold?

Show your working

| litres |

2 marks

18 A bag contains 375 raisins.

16 children each take the same number of raisins from the bag.

There are 7 raisins left in the bag.

How many raisins did each child take?

Show your working

| raisins |

2 marks

19 A bakery sold **300** tarts in January.
The pie chart shows the different flavours of tart that were sold.

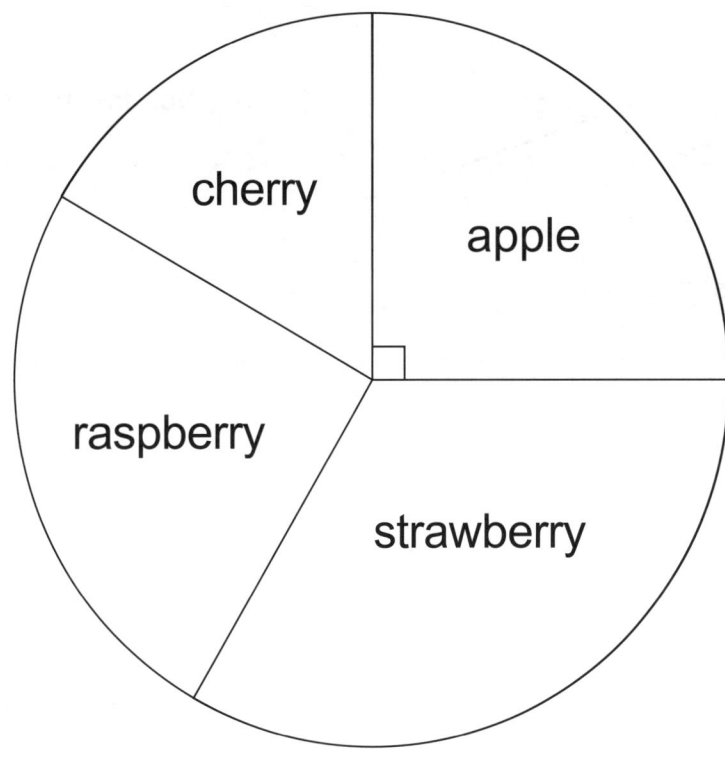

How many apple tarts were sold in January?

1 mark

What fraction of the tarts sold were cherry?
Use a protractor (angle measurer) to help find your answer.

1 mark

20 Two triangles meet at a vertex.
The grey triangle is **isosceles**.

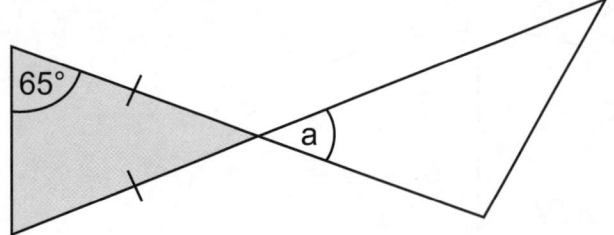

Not drawn to scale.

What is the size of angle a?

Show your working

°

2 marks

21 Juan is sending out 102 party invitations. He buys a stamp for each invitation.

A pack of six stamps costs £3.30.

Juan pays with three twenty pound notes.

How much change does Juan get?

Show your working

3 marks

MHP26U

Key Stage Two Mathematics

Set B
Paper 3: Reasoning

Calculator Not Allowed

40 minutes

First name	
Middle name	
Last name	
School	

Date of birth	Day		Month		Year	

Total marks

1 Round **3685** to the nearest **ten**.

1 mark

Round **11645** to the nearest **thousand**.

1 mark

2 A school is putting on a play. The play starts at 6.30 pm.

Amy arrives 13 minutes before the start of the play.

What time does Amy arrive? Give your answer using the **24-hour clock**.

1 mark

The play finishes at 9.12 pm.

How long is the play?

	hours and		minutes

1 mark

3 Mrs Truman runs a coffee shop.

The pictogram shows how many cups of coffee she makes in a day.

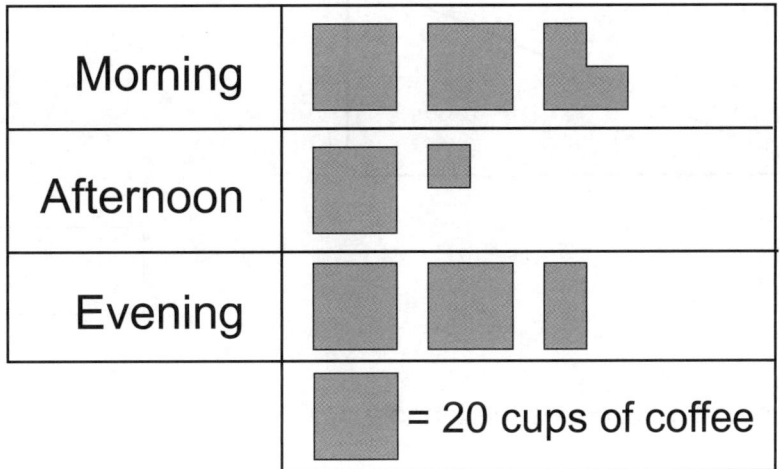

How many cups did she make in **total**?

1 mark

How many **more** cups did she make in the evening than the afternoon?

1 mark

4 Circle the number that represents the value of the **2** in **9 247 683**.

Two hundred   Two thousand   Twenty thousand

Two hundred thousand   Two million

1 mark

5 Use a protractor (angle measurer) to find the size of the **smallest** angle in this triangle.

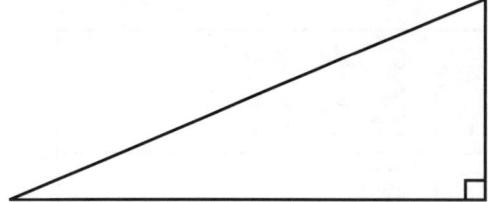

°

1 mark

Circle the word that describes the triangle.

Isosceles   Right-angled   Equilateral

1 mark

6 Here is a floor plan of a room.

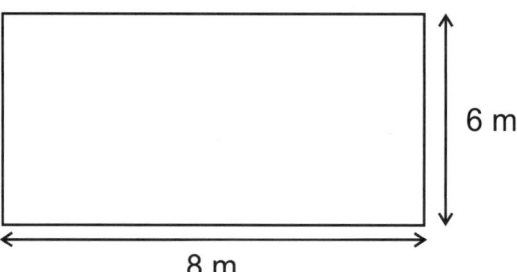

6 m

8 m

Carpet costs £4 per m².

How much would it cost to carpet this room?

Show your working

2 marks

7 Fill in the gaps to make this multiplication correct.

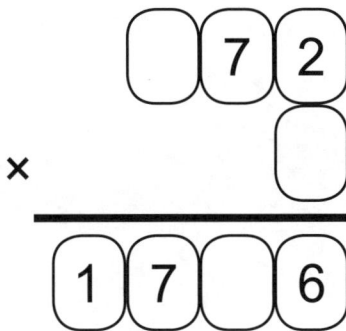

$$\begin{array}{r} \boxed{}\,\boxed{7}\,\boxed{2} \\ \times \quad \boxed{} \\ \hline \boxed{1}\,\boxed{7}\,\boxed{}\,\boxed{6} \end{array}$$

2 marks

8 What is the perimeter of this shape?

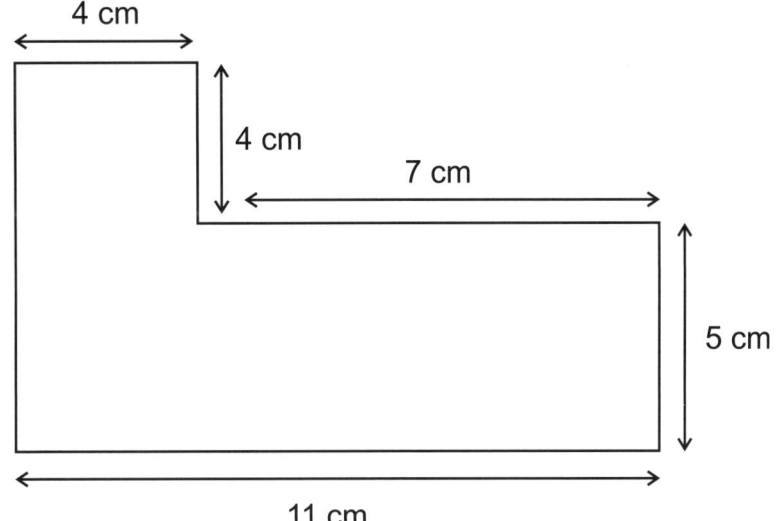

4 cm

4 cm

7 cm

5 cm

11 cm

cm

1 mark

9 Write $\frac{101}{1000}$ as a decimal.

1 mark

10 A bus ticket costs £2.40 for an adult.
A child's ticket is half price.
6 children and 1 adult buy bus tickets.

What is the total cost of the tickets?

Show your working

2 marks

11   A bar of chocolate is made up of 12 identical pieces. It weighs 72g.

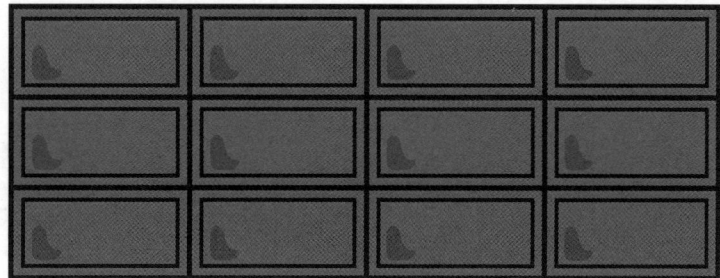

Alice eats 5 pieces.

What is the weight of the chocolate that is left?

Show
your
working

g

2 marks

12   Circle **one fraction** and **one decimal** that add together to make **0.5**.

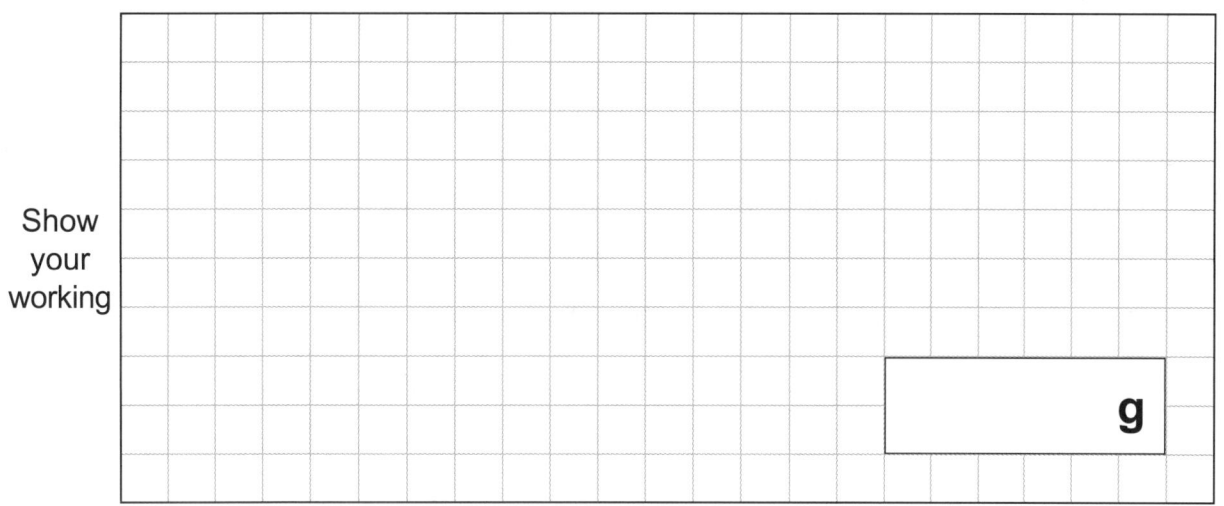

1 mark

A carton of milk has the shape of a cuboid.

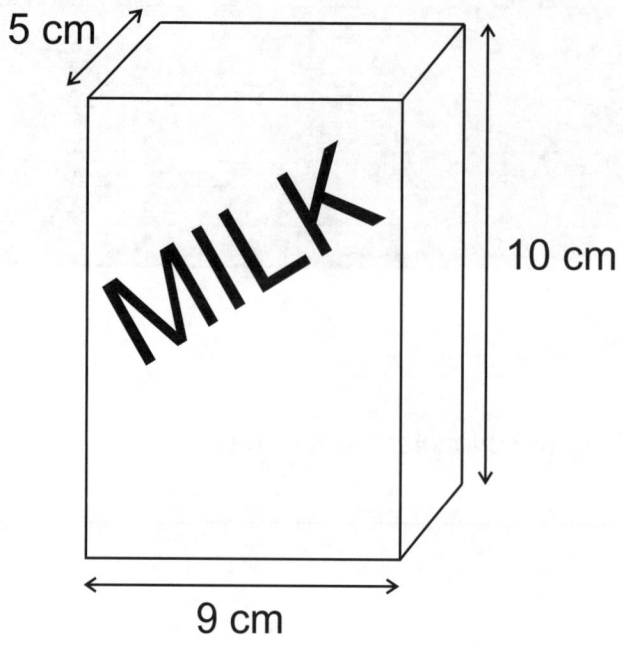

5 cm

10 cm

9 cm

Billy drinks **150 cm³** of milk each day.

How many days does it take him to drink the whole carton?

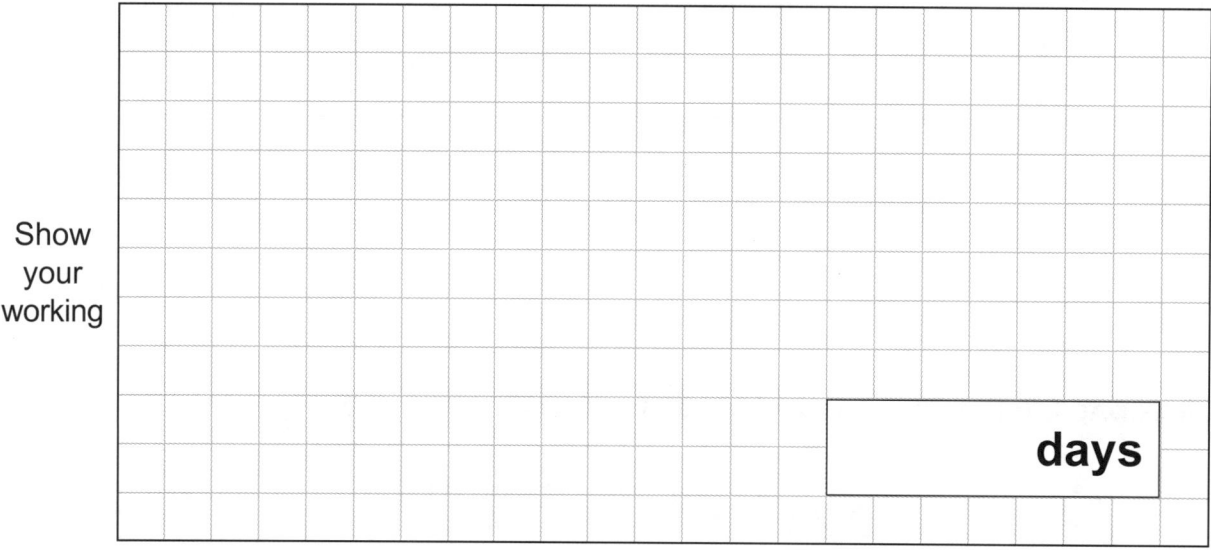

Show your working

days

2 marks

14 Here is a multiplication.

$$99 \times 101$$

Explain how you can find the answer to this **without** using a written multiplication method.

1 mark

Write down the answer to the multiplication.

1 mark

15 Mrs Truman has 50 fish in her pond.
40% of them are green.
18 of them are red.
The rest are brown.

What **fraction** of the fish are brown?

Show
your
working

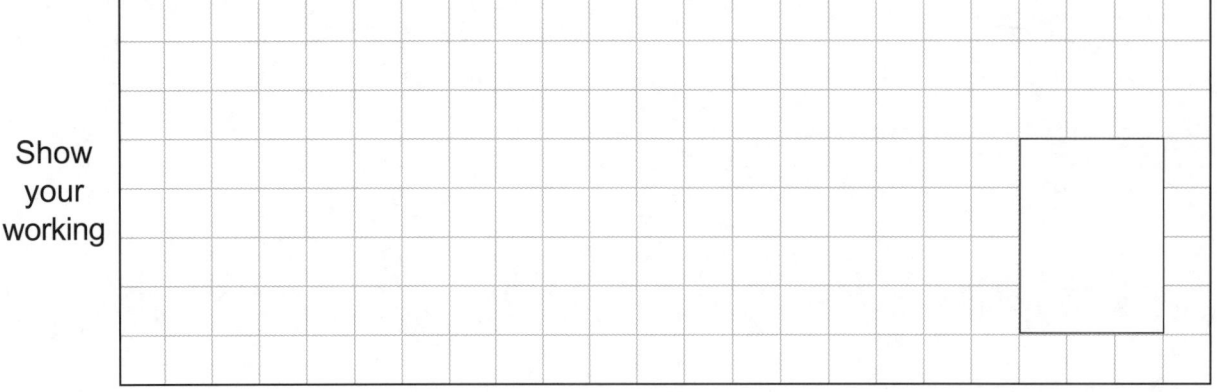

2 marks

16 Jimmy is playing a game. He follows these instructions to work out his score.

1. Roll a dice
2. Multiply the number by 6
3. Subtract 10

Jimmy gets a score of **20**.

What number did he roll?

1 mark

He rolls the dice again and gets a score that is **less than 0**.

What number did he roll?

1 mark

17 What is the largest common factor of 63 and 28?

1 mark

18 Kishan is thinking of **two** numbers. He calls them P and Q.
He says "If you multiply P by 10 and then add 3 you get Q".

Circle the equation that shows how P and Q are linked.

$Q = 3P + 10$ $\qquad$ $Q = 10P + 3$ $\qquad$ $Q + 3 = 10P$

$P + 3 = 10Q$ $\qquad$ $P = 10Q + 3$

1 mark

Write down **two** possible sets of values for P and Q.

P = ☐ $\qquad$ Q = ☐

P = ☐ $\qquad$ Q = ☐

1 mark

19 Tom has a bag of compost. He puts 3.6 kg of compost on his flower bed.

He puts 4.75 kg of compost on his vegetable patch.

He still has $\frac{4}{5}$ of the bag of compost left over.

How many kilograms of compost were in the bag to start with?

Show your working

| | kg |

2 marks

20 The **radius** of the circle below is **3**.

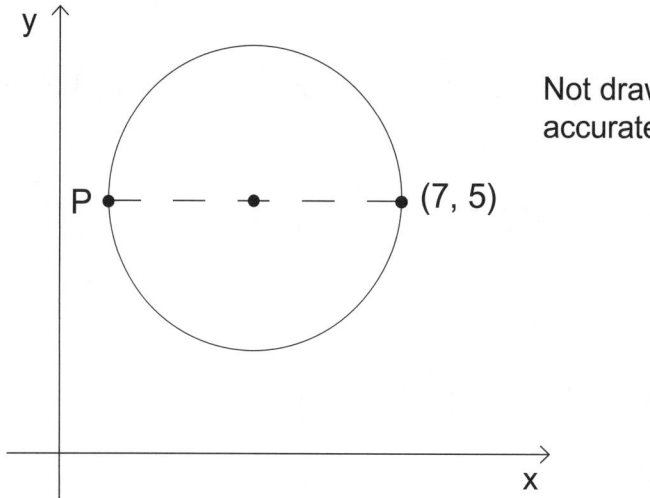

Not drawn accurately.

What is the diameter of the circle?

1 mark

What are the coordinates of point P?

(,)

1 mark

MHP26U

Key Stage Two

Mathematics

SATS Practice Papers

Instructions with Answers & Mark Scheme

Contents

Published by CGP

Editors:
Izzy Bowen, Chris Corrall, Ruth Wilbourne

Many thanks to Alison Griffin and Karen Wells for proofreading.
Also thanks to Jan Greenway for the copyright research.

Coin images Set A, Paper 3, p.4:
two pound coin, 50 pence coins and 5 pence coin © iStock.com/duncan1890
one pound coins © iStock.com/LPETTET
20 pence coins © iStock.com/Jaap2
2 pence coins © iStock.com/peterspiro
1 pence coin © iStock.com/coopder1

Clipart from Corel®
Printed by Zenith Print & Packaging Ltd, Pontypridd.

Text, design, layout and original illustrations
© Coordination Group Publications Ltd. (CGP) 2020
All rights reserved.

National Curriculum references on pages 5 and 6 reproduced under the terms of the Open Government Licence v3.0.
http://www.nationalarchives.gov.uk/doc/open-government-licence/version/3/

Photocopying more than 5% of a paper is not permitted, even if you have a CLA licence.
Extra copies are available from CGP with next day delivery   •   0800 1712 712   •   www.cgpbooks.co.uk

There are two sets of practice papers in this pack

Each **set** has:

Paper 1: Arithmetic
30 minute test
no calculators allowed   **40 marks**

Paper 2: Reasoning
40 minute test
no calculators allowed   **35 marks**

Paper 3: Reasoning
40 minute test
no calculators allowed   **35 marks**

Make sure they have these things

For all the papers:
A **pen** and a **pencil**.
A **rubber**.

For papers 2 and 3 only:
A **ruler**.
A **protractor** (angle measurer).
A **mirror**.

Doing the papers

1) The most important thing is to **understand** the questions.
    Encourage them to read everything really **carefully** so they know exactly what to do.

2) Some questions will ask them to show their working.

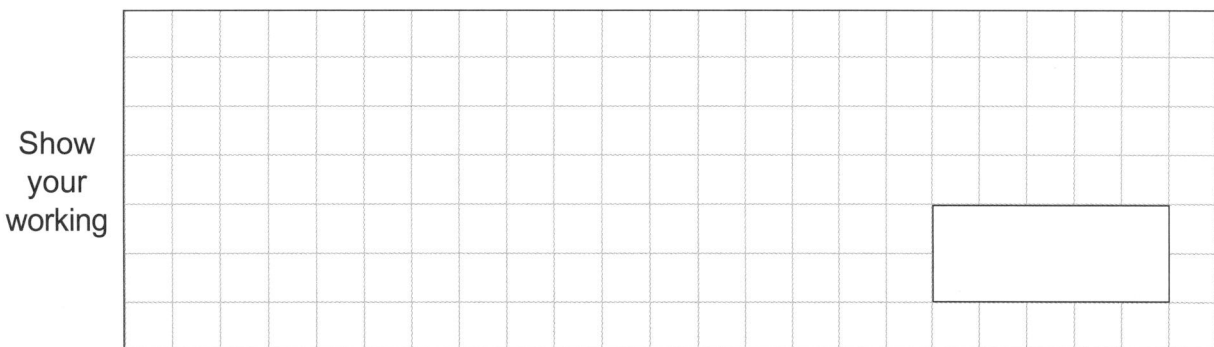

Show
your
working

They need to do all their **working** on the **grid**, then write the **final answer** in the **box**.
Even if they get the answer **wrong**, they might get marks for trying to do the question
in the **right way**.

How to Mark the Papers

Use the answers in this booklet to mark each paper, then write the scores in the table below. For each set, add up the scores for Paper 1, Paper 2 and Paper 3 to get a **mark out of 110.**

	Paper 1 mark out of 40		**Paper 2** mark out of 35		**Paper 3** mark out of 35		**TOTAL** mark out of 110
Set A		+		+		=	_____
Set B		+		+		=	_____

The scores for these practice papers will give you a pretty good idea of whether a child is working at the **expected standard** in **Maths**.

The mark needed to achieve the **expected standard** varies from year to year, but if they get **60** or more **out of 110** then they should be on track.

Content Domain Coverage

The mark schemes in this Answer Book refer to the content domain references as they appear in the Standards & Testing Agency's 'Mathematics test framework' document.

Qu.	Answer	Marking notes	Marks (Domain)
1	13 400, 14 499, 95 782, 134 500, 195 287		**1** (5N2)

These refer to elements of the National Curriculum Programme of Study, which is split by Year.

For example, '5N2' refers to Year 5, substrand N2 ('read, write, order and compare numbers').

You will see in the mark scheme that some substrands are divided further. For example, 'N3a' refers to 'place value', while 'N3b' refers to 'roman numerals'.

For a detailed breakdown on the content of each year's substrands, please visit the 'Mathematics test framework' document on the STA website.

Content Domain Coverage

This table sets out the areas of the content domain that are assessed in these papers.

Topic	Sub-strand	Ref	Set A			Set B		
			Paper 1	Paper 2	Paper 3	Paper 1	Paper 2	Paper 3
Number and place value	counting (in multiples)	N1					Q1	
	read, write, order and compare numbers	N2	Q1	Q4				
	place value; roman numerals	N3			Q14			Q4
	identify, represent and estimate; rounding	N4					Q1	
	negative numbers	N5		Q5			Q14	
	number problems	N6						
Addition, subtraction, multiplication and division (calculations)	add / subtract mentally	C1	Q3					
	add / subtract using written methods	C2	Q7, 10, 16, 20	Q6		Q3, 4, 8, 10, 16, 21		
	estimate, use inverses and check	C3			Q13			
	add / subtract to solve problems	C4						
	properties of number (multiples, factors, primes, squares and cubes)	C5		Q9	Q9, 14		Q3, 15	Q17
	multiply / divide mentally	C6	Q4, 5, 6, 9, 11, 21			Q1, 2, 5, 7, 9, 12, 15, 22		Q9, 14
	multiply / divide using written methods	C7	Q2, 8, 12, 13, 17, 23, 25, 27, 30, 33			Q11, 13, 24, 27, 32, 33	Q9	Q7
	solve problems (commutative, associative, distributive and all four operations)	C8		Q2, 10, 15, 20			Q4, 18, 21	Q6, 10, 14, 16
	order of operations	C9	Q22, 36		Q20	Q20, 36		
Fractions, decimals and percentages	recognise, find, write, name and count fractions	F1						
	equivalent fractions	F2		Q17			Q10, 12	
	comparing and ordering fractions	F3						
	add / subtract fractions	F4	Q18, 28, 35	Q17		Q19, 25, 31, 34	Q12	
	multiply / divide fractions	F5	Q32, 34		Q18	Q26, 28, 35		
	fractions / decimals equivalence	F6			Q2			Q9
	rounding decimals	F7						
	compare and order decimals	F8	Q14, 15, 19, 29	Q7		Q6, 14, 18, 23	Q5, 13	
	multiply / divide decimals	F9	Q24			Q29		
	solve problems with fractions and decimals	F10			Q12, 15			Q19
	fractions / decimal / percentage equivalence	F11						Q12, 15
	solve problems with percentages	F12						

Content Domain Coverage

Topic	Sub-strand	Ref	Set A			Set B		
			Paper 1	Paper 2	Paper 3	Paper 1	Paper 2	Paper 3
Ratio and proportion	relative sizes, similarity	R1		Q13	Q19			Q11
	use of percentages for comparison	R2	Q26, 31			Q17, 30		Q15
	scale factors	R3						
	unequal sharing and grouping	R4			Q17		Q17	
Algebra	missing number problems expressed in algebra	A1						
	simple formulae expressed in words	A2		Q11	Q11		Q11	Q18
	generate and describe linear number sequences	A3			Q6			
	number sentences involving two unknowns	A4						Q18
	enumerate all possibilities of combinations of two variables	A5						
Measurement	compare, describe and order measures	M1						
	estimate, measure and read scales	M2		Q3				
	money	M3						
	telling time, ordering time, duration and units of time	M4			Q4		Q6	Q2
	convert between metric units	M5			Q17		Q9	
	convert metric / imperial	M6	Q19					
	perimeter, area	M7		Q14, 16			Q7	Q6, 8
	volume	M8						Q13
	solve problems (a, money; b, length; c, mass / weight; d, capacity / volume)	M9		Q13	Q5		Q8, 21	Q10, 13
Geometry — properties of shapes	recognise and name common shapes	G1						
	describe properties and classify shapes	G2		Q1, 8				Q5
	draw and make shapes and relate 2-D to 3-D shapes (including nets)	G3			Q3			
	angles – measuring and properties	G4		Q18	Q7, 16		Q20	Q5
	circles	G5						Q20
Geometry — position and direction	patterns	P1						
	describe position, direction and movement	P2			Q10			
	co-ordinates	P3		Q8			Q16	Q20
Statistics	interpret and represent data	S1			Q8		Q2, 19	
	solve problems involving data	S2			Q1		Q2	Q3
	mean average	S3		Q12				

Set A – Answers

Set A Paper 1

Qu.	Answer	Marking notes	Marks (Domain)
1	4941		1 (3N2b)
2	148		1 (3C7)
3	364		1 (3C1)
4	11		1 (3C6)
5	730		1 (4C6b)
6	240		1 (4C6b)
7	$\begin{array}{r} 7\ 6\ 9\ 8\ 5 \\ +\ \ \ 5\ 2\ 3\ 6 \\ \hline 8\ 2\ 2\ 2\ 1 \\ {\scriptstyle 1\ 1\ 1\ 1} \end{array}$		1 (5C2)
8	225		1 (3C7)
9	1600		1 (5C6a)
10	795		1 (3C2)
11	86 600		1 (5C6b)
12	$\begin{array}{r} 5\ 4\ 6 \\ \times\ \ \ \ \ 4 \\ \hline 2\ 1\ 8\ 4 \\ {\scriptstyle 1\ 2} \end{array}$		1 (4C7)
13	657		1 (4C7)
14	$\begin{array}{r} 7.6\ 5 \\ -\ \ 6.5\ 4 \\ \hline 1.1\ 1 \end{array}$		1 (4F8)
15	$\begin{array}{r} 1\ 3.7\ 7\ 7 \\ +\ \ \ 9.4\ 6\ 0 \\ \hline 2\ 3.2\ 3\ 7 \\ {\scriptstyle 1\ 1\ 1} \end{array}$		1 (5F8)
16	76 293		1 (5C2)
17	$\begin{array}{r} 7\ 8\ 2 \\ 7\overline{\smash{\big)}5\ 4\ ^5 7\ ^1 4} \end{array}$		1 (5C7b)
18	$\frac{2}{7} + \frac{4}{7} = \frac{2+4}{7} = \frac{6}{7}$		1 (3F4)
19	$\begin{array}{r} ^4 \cancel{5}\ ^{14}\cancel{5}.^9\cancel{0}\ ^{1}0 \\ -\ \ \ \ 5.7\ 2 \\ \hline 4\ 9.2\ 8 \end{array}$		1 (5F8)
20	$\begin{array}{r} ^4\cancel{5}\ ^1 6\ ^8\cancel{9}\ 8\ ^8\cancel{9}\ ^8\cancel{9} \\ -\ \ \ 7\ 0\ 9\ 1\ 9 \\ \hline 4\ 9\ 8\ 9\ 7\ 9 \end{array}$		1 (5C2)
21	0.0015		1 (5C6b)
22	$2^3 + 2 = 8 + 2 = \mathbf{10}$		1 (6C9)
23	$\begin{array}{r} 2\ 1\ 0 \\ 11\overline{\smash{\big)}2\ 3\ ^1 1\ 0} \end{array}$		1 (6C7b)
24	$10 \times 7.4 = 74,\ 2 \times 7.4 = 14.8$ So, $12 \times 7.4 = 74 + 14.8 = \mathbf{88.8}$		1 (6F9b)

Qu.	Answer	Marking notes	Marks (Domain)
25	$\begin{array}{r} 6\ 6\ 4 \\ \times\ \ \ \ 3\ 4 \\ \hline 2\ 6\ 5\ 6 \\ {\scriptstyle 2\ 1} \\ 1\ 9\ 9\ 2\ 0 \\ {\scriptstyle 2\ 1} \\ \hline 2\ 2\ 5\ 7\ 6 \\ {\scriptstyle 1\ 1} \end{array}$	2 marks for the correct answer, otherwise 1 mark for the correct method with no more than one error. Award no marks if the error is the placing of digits in incorrect columns.	2 (5C7a)
26	10% of 2400 = 2400 ÷ 10 = 240 20% of 2400 = 240 × 2 = **480**		1 (6R2)
27	$\begin{array}{r} 2\ 5 \\ 39\overline{\smash{\big)}9\ 7\ 5} \\ -\ 7\ 8 \\ \hline 1\ 9\ 5 \\ -\ 1\ 9\ 5 \\ \hline 0 \end{array}$	2 marks for the correct answer, otherwise 1 mark for the correct method with no more than one error.	2 (6C7b)
28	$\frac{5}{6} + 1\frac{1}{12} = \frac{10}{12} + \frac{13}{12}$ $= \frac{10+13}{12} = \mathbf{\frac{23}{12}}$ or $\mathbf{1\frac{11}{12}}$		1 (6F4)
29	$\begin{array}{r} \cancel{1}\ ^{15}\cancel{6}.^{11}\cancel{2}\ ^{15}\cancel{5}\ 3 \\ -\ \ 7.3\ 6\ 0 \\ \hline 8.8\ 9\ 3 \end{array}$		1 (5F8)
30	$\begin{array}{r} 4\ 9\ 2\ 2 \\ \times\ \ \ \ \ \ 7\ 7 \\ \hline 3\ 4\ 4\ 5\ 4 \\ {\scriptstyle 6\ 1\ 1} \\ 3\ 4\ 4\ 5\ 4\ 0 \\ {\scriptstyle 6\ 1\ 1} \\ \hline 3\ 7\ 8\ 9\ 9\ 4 \end{array}$	2 marks for the correct answer, otherwise 1 mark for the correct method with no more than one error. Award no marks if the error is the placing of digits in incorrect columns.	2 (5C7a)
31	10% of 350 = 350 ÷ 10 = 35 20% of 350 = 35 × 2 = 70 1% of 350 = 35 ÷ 10 = 3.5 2% of 350 = 3.5 × 2 = 7 So, 22% of 350 = 70 + 7 = **77**		1 (6R2)
32	$\frac{1}{2} \times \frac{2}{3} = \frac{1 \times 2}{2 \times 3} = \mathbf{\frac{2}{6}}$ or $\mathbf{\frac{1}{3}}$		1 (6F5a)
33	$\begin{array}{r} 1\ 5\ 3 \\ 45\overline{\smash{\big)}6\ 8\ 8\ 5} \\ -\ 4\ 5 \\ \hline 2\ 3\ 8 \\ -\ 2\ 2\ 5 \\ \hline 1\ 3\ 5 \\ -\ 1\ 3\ 5 \\ \hline 0 \end{array}$	2 marks for the correct answer, otherwise 1 mark for the correct method with no more than one error.	2 (6C7b)
34	$\frac{7}{10} \div 9 = \frac{7}{10 \times 9} = \mathbf{\frac{7}{90}}$		1 (6F5b)
35	$\frac{1}{4} + \frac{4}{5} = \frac{5}{20} + \frac{16}{20} = \frac{5+16}{20}$ $= \mathbf{\frac{21}{20}}$ or $\mathbf{1\frac{1}{20}}$		1 (6F4)
36	$44 + 72 \div 12 = 44 + 6 = \mathbf{50}$		1 (6C9)

Set A – Answers

Set A Paper 2

Qu.	Answer	Marking notes	Marks (Domain)
1a			1 (4G2b)
1b			1 (4G2c)
2	He bought 6 × 22 = 132 slices of bread. So, he has 132 – 120 = **12** slices of bread left over.	2 marks for the correct answer, otherwise 1 mark for a correct method.	2 (4C8)
3a	27 ml – 12 ml = **15 ml**		1 (3M2c)
3b			1 (3M2c)
4	March, June, April, May		1 (6N2)
5a	Tom		1 (5N5/6N5)
5b	4		1 (5N5/6N5)
6	In the standard format, the subtraction would be written as: $\begin{array}{r} {}^4\!\,5\,{}^1\!2\,\,9 \\ -\,3\,7\,4 \\ \hline 1\,5\,5 \end{array}$	2 marks for all three digits correct, otherwise 1 mark for two digits correct.	2 (4C2)
7a	5.22		1 (5F8)
7b	5.525 – 5.22 = **0.305**		1 (5F8)
8	The shape is a **pentagon**. It is **irregular**.	1 mark for 'pentagon', 1 mark for 'irregular'.	2 (4P3b/5G2b)
9a	7		1 (5C5a)
9b	121		1 (5C5a)
10	The total number of custard pies needed is 17 × 5 = 85. Each pie needs 35 ml of cream: $\begin{array}{r} 8\,5 \\ \times\quad 3\,5 \\ \hline 4\,2\,5 \\ 2\,5\,5\,0 \\ \hline 2\,9\,7\,5 \end{array}$ So, that's **2975 ml** of cream.	2 marks for the correct answer, otherwise 1 mark for a correct method.	2 (5C8a)

Qu.	Answer	Marking notes	Marks (Domain)
11	△ + ☆ = 40, so ☆ + △ = 40 This means ◯ + ◯ + 40 = 72, so ◯ + ◯ = 72 – 40 = 32. So, ◯ = 32 ÷ 2 = **16**.	2 marks for the correct answer, otherwise 1 mark for a correct method.	2 (6A2)
12	(15 + 12 + 24 + 9) ÷ 4 = **15 kg**		1 (6S3)
13	8 mangoes cost £1.25 × 8 = £10 One pineapple costs £10 ÷ 5 = **£2**.	2 marks for the correct answer, otherwise 1 mark for a correct method.	2 (6R1/ 5M9a)
14	The height of the rectangle is 96 ÷ 12 = 8. So, the area of the triangle is $\frac{1}{2}$ × 10 × 8 = **40 cm²**.	2 marks for the correct answer, otherwise 1 mark for a correct method.	2 (6M7b)
15	2.5 × 4 = 10, so 2.5 × 40 = 100		1 (6C8)
16	The end of the pool is an equilateral triangle, so all of its sides are the same length. This means the vertical height of the rectangular part of the pool is 12.7 m. So, the perimeter of the pool is 25.4 + 25.4 + 12.7 + 12.7 + 12.7 = 50.8 + 38.1 = **88.9 m**.	2 marks for the correct answer, otherwise 1 mark for correctly identifying the length of each side of the shape.	2 (5M7a)
17	⑥⁄₇ ⁵⁄₇ ¹¹⁄₇ ④⁄₇ 1¹⁄₇ 1²⁄₇		1 (5F2a/ 6F4)
18	E.g. A parallelogram has two pairs of equal angles. So if A is 130° and B is 70° then the angles inside the parallelogram would add up to 400°. This is impossible, as the angles in a quadrilateral add up to 360°. So Mina must be wrong.		1 (6G4a)
19	8 km ≈ 5 miles 96 ÷ 8 × 5 = 12 × 5 = **60 miles**		1 (6M6)
20	$\begin{array}{r} 2\,5\,5 \\ \times\quad 6 \\ \hline 1\,5\,3\,0 \\ {}_3\,{}_3 \end{array}$ So, the books weigh 1530 g. 20 pens is 20 ÷ 5 = 4 sets. This weighs 4 × 30 g = 120 g. So there's 1530 g + 120 g = 1650 g in the parcel so far. 2 kg = 2000 g, so the rubbers can weigh up to 2000 g – 1650 g = 350 g. 350 ÷ 20 = 35 ÷ 2 = 17 remainder 1, so Aziza can send **17 rubbers**.	3 marks for the correct answer. Otherwise, 2 marks for finding 1650 g, or for a correct method with no more than one error. 1 mark for a correct method with more than one error.	3 (6C8)

© CGP 2020

Set A – Answers

Set A Paper 3

Qu.	Answer	Marking notes	Marks (Domain)
1a	$\begin{array}{r} 9\ 5\ 6\ 2 \\ +\ \ 8\ 7\ 2\ 1 \\ \hline 1\ 8\ 2\ 8\ 3 \\ \hline \end{array}$		1 (4S2)
1b	$\begin{array}{r} \cancel{9}\ \cancel{5}\ \cancel{6}\ 2 \\ -\ 7\ 8\ 8\ 8 \\ \hline 1\ 6\ 7\ 4 \\ \hline \end{array}$ (with borrowing: 8, 14, 15, 1)		1 (4S2)
2	0.83		1 (4F6b)
3			1 (6G3b)
4a	$60 \times 8 = \textbf{480 seconds}$		1 (3M4e)
4b	$24 \times 3 = \textbf{72 hours}$		1 (3M4e)
5	Tom has £3.75, Aziza has £2.15. Together they have £5.90, so they need another **£4.10**.	2 marks for the correct answer, otherwise 1 mark for a correct method.	2 (5M9a)
6	27, 46, 65, **84**, **103** (The rule for the sequence is 'add 19'.)		1 (6A3)
7	Reflex Acute Obtuse (matching) 2 marks for all three angles matched correctly, otherwise 1 mark for one angle matched correctly.		2 (4G4)
8a	19 minutes		1 (5S1)
8b	14:05		1 (5S1)
9	The only even prime is 2. So the number is $2 \times 3 \times 5 = \textbf{30}$.		1 (5C5b)
10	✔		1 (5P2)
11a	$a = 2 \times b = 2 \times 44 = \textbf{88}$		1 (6A2)
11b	$5c = 75 - 50 = 25$ So $c = 25 \div 5 = \textbf{5}$		1 (6A2)
12	$4 \times 250 = 1000$ ml $\frac{2}{5} \times 1000 = \frac{2 \times 1000}{5}$ $= \frac{2000}{5} = \textbf{400 ml}$	2 marks for the correct answer, otherwise 1 mark for a correct method.	2 (4F10a)

Qu.	Answer	Marking notes	Marks (Domain)
13a	$6 \times 50\ 000 = 300\ 000$		1 (6C3)
13b	You would expect the estimate to be more than the actual answer as you have rounded both the numbers up.		1 (6C3)
14	less than 64 — XXV; square number — LXIV; more than 64 — XC. 2 marks for all three Roman numerals in the correct positions, otherwise 1 mark for two numerals in the correct positions.		2 (5C5d/ 4N3b)
15	height of drawers $= 2 \times$ height of desk $= 2 \times 0.7$ m $= 1.4$ m height of wardrobe $=$ height of drawers $+ 0.5$ m $= 1.4$ m $+ 0.5$ m $= \textbf{1.9 m}$	2 marks for the correct answer, otherwise 1 mark for a correct method.	2 (5F10)
16	The angles inside a triangle add up to 180°, so the missing angle inside the triangle is $180° - (75° + 50°)$ $= 180° - 125° = 55°$. Angle a and this angle make a straight line, so $a = 180° - 55° = \textbf{125°}$.	2 marks for the correct answer, otherwise 1 mark for a correct method.	2 (6G4a/ 6G4b)
17	4 kg $= 4000$ g $4000 \div 80 = 40 \div 8 = 50$, so 4000 g of ice cream needs $25 \times 50 = 125 \times 10$ $= 1250$ ml of syrup. 1250 ml $= \textbf{1.25 litres}$	2 marks for the correct answer, otherwise 1 mark for a correct method.	2 (6M5/ 6R4)
18a	$\frac{5}{6} \div 3 = \frac{5}{18}$		1 (6F5a/ 6F5b)
18b	$\frac{2}{3} \times \frac{6}{7} = \frac{4}{7}$		1 (6F5a/ 6F5b)
19	Kishan has $1 - \frac{5}{7} = \frac{2}{7}$ of the swim still to do. $\frac{2}{7}$ of the swim $= 100$ m, so $\frac{1}{7}$ is 50 m. So the sponsored swim is 7×50 m $= \textbf{350 m}$ long.	2 marks for the correct answer, otherwise 1 mark for a correct method.	2 (6R1)
20	$5 \times (7 - 3) + 4 = 24$ $(6 - 3) \times (4 + 8) = 36$	1 mark for each correct calculation.	2 (6C9)

KS2 Maths — Answers & Mark Scheme

© CGP 2020

Set B – Answers

Set B Paper 1

Qu.	Answer	Marking notes	Marks (Domain)
1	$5 \times 3 = 15$, so $50 \times 3 =$ **150**		1 (3C6)
2	1		1 (4C6b)
3	2105		1 (4C2)
4	421		1 (3C2)
5	88		1 (3C6)
6	2		1 (4F8)
7	12		1 (3C6)
8	$\begin{array}{r} 7\,0\,0\,0\,6 \\ +\ \ 7\,9\,9\,5 \\ \hline 7\,8\,0\,0\,1 \\ {\scriptstyle 1\ \ 1\ \ 1} \end{array}$		1 (5C2)
9	$8 \times 7 = 56$ $80 \times 70 = 8 \times 7 \times 100 =$ **5600**		1 (5C6a)
10	29 200		1 (5C2)
11	$\begin{array}{r} 7\,4\,6 \\ \times\ \ \ \ 5 \\ \hline 3\,7\,3\,0 \\ {\scriptstyle 2\ 3} \end{array}$		1 (4C7)
12	89 000		1 (5C6b)
13	$6\,\overline{\smash{\big)}\,5\,8\,{}^{4}2}$ gives **9 7**		1 (5C7b)
14	$\begin{array}{r} 2\,0.0\,0\,2 \\ +\ \ 1.1\,8\,0 \\ \hline 2\,1.1\,8\,2 \end{array}$		1 (5F8)
15	0.36		1 (5C6b)
16	$\begin{array}{r} {}^{2}\cancel{3}\,{}^{9}\cancel{0}\,{}^{1}\cancel{0}\,{}^{1}2\,1\,6 \\ -\ \ \ \ 5\,4\,9\,2 \\ \hline 2\,4\,7\,2\,4 \end{array}$		1 (5C2)
17	10% of $640 = 640 \div 10 =$ **64**		1 (6R2)
18	$\begin{array}{r} 3\,3\,3.3\,6 \\ -\ \ \ \ 2\,1.2\,1 \\ \hline 3\,1\,2.1\,5 \end{array}$		1 (5F8)
19	$\frac{11}{13} - \frac{5}{13} = \frac{11-5}{13} = \frac{\mathbf{6}}{\mathbf{13}}$		1 (3F4)
20	$5^2 + 5 = 25 + 5 =$ **30**		1 (6C9)
21	$\begin{array}{r} 6\,{}^{7}\cancel{8}\,{}^{9}\cancel{0}\,{}^{14}\cancel{5}\,{}^{10}\cancel{0}\,{}^{1}1 \\ -\ \ \ 1\,2\,6\,8\,9 \\ \hline 6\,6\,7\,8\,1\,2 \end{array}$		1 (5C2)
22	$84 \div 12 = 7$ So, $8400 \div 12 = 7 \times 100 =$ **700**		1 (5C6a)
23	3.65		1 (5F8)
24	$\begin{array}{r} 5\,9 \\ \times\ \ \ 5\,2 \\ \hline 1\,1\,8 \\ 2\,{}^{4}9\,5\,0 \\ \hline 3\,0\,6\,8 \\ {\scriptstyle 1} \end{array}$	2 marks for the correct answer, otherwise 1 mark for the correct method with no more than one error. Award no marks if the error is the placing of digits in incorrect columns.	2 (5C7a)
25	$1\frac{2}{3} + \frac{2}{3} = \frac{5}{3} + \frac{2}{3} = \frac{5+2}{3} = \frac{\mathbf{7}}{\mathbf{3}}$ or $2\frac{\mathbf{1}}{\mathbf{3}}$		1 (6F4)
26	$\frac{1}{6} \times \frac{1}{7} = \frac{1}{6 \times 7} = \frac{\mathbf{1}}{\mathbf{42}}$		1 (6F5a)
27	$\begin{array}{r} 3\,5 \\ 17\,\overline{\smash{\big)}\,5\,9\,5} \\ -\,5\,1 \\ \hline 8\,5 \\ -\,8\,5 \\ \hline 0 \end{array}$	2 marks for the correct answer, otherwise 1 mark for a correct method with no more than one error.	2 (6C7b)
28	$15 \times \frac{3}{5} = \frac{15 \times 3}{5} = \frac{45}{5} = \mathbf{9}$		1 (5F5)
29	$10 \times 5.6 = 56$ $3 \times 5.6 = 16.8$ So, $13 \times 5.6 = 56 + 16.8 =$ **72.8**		1 (6F9b)
30	10% of $80 = 80 \div 10 = 8$ 80% of $80 = 8 \times 8 = 64$ 5% of $80 = 8 \div 2 = 4$ So, 85% of $80 = 64 + 4 =$ **68**		1 (6R2)
31	$\frac{13}{14} + \frac{1}{28} = \frac{26}{28} + \frac{1}{28} = \frac{26+1}{28} = \frac{\mathbf{27}}{\mathbf{28}}$		1 (5F4)
32	$\begin{array}{r} 3\,7\,8\,4 \\ \times\ \ \ \ \ \ 2\,6 \\ \hline 2\,2\,7\,0\,4 \\ {\scriptstyle 4\ 5\ 2} \\ +\ 7\,5\,6\,8\,0 \\ \hline 9\,8\,3\,8\,4 \\ {\scriptstyle 1} \end{array}$	2 marks for the correct answer, otherwise 1 mark for the correct method with no more than one error. Award no marks if the error is the placing of digits in incorrect columns.	2 (6C7a)
33	$\begin{array}{r} 7\,3 \\ 37\,\overline{\smash{\big)}\,2\,7\,0\,1} \\ -\,2\,5\,9 \\ \hline 1\,1\,1 \\ -\,1\,1\,1 \\ \hline 0 \end{array}$	2 marks for the correct answer, otherwise 1 mark for a correct method with no more than one error.	2 (6C7b)
34	$1\frac{2}{3} - \frac{3}{4} = \frac{5}{3} - \frac{3}{4} = \frac{20}{12} - \frac{9}{12} = \frac{\mathbf{11}}{\mathbf{12}}$		1 (6F4)
35	$\frac{4}{5} \div 5 = \frac{4}{5 \times 5} = \frac{\mathbf{4}}{\mathbf{25}}$		1 (6F5b)
36	$(10 - 2) + 14 \times 2 = 8 + 14 \times 2$ $= 8 + 28 =$ **36**		1 (6C9)

Set B – Answers

Set B Paper 2

Qu.	Answer	Marking notes	Marks (Domain)
1	45 294, 35 294, 25 294, **15 294, 5294**		1 (5N1)
2a			1 (3S1)
2b	5 + 8 + 11 = **24** children		1 (3S2)
3	**19** and **5**, or **17** and **7**, or **13** and **11**		1 (5C5c)
4a	$\begin{array}{r} 3\ 1\ 7\ 6\ 5 \\ +\ 1\ 8\ 9\ 9\ 9 \\ \hline £5\ 0\ 7\ 6\ 4 \end{array}$		1 (5C8b)
4b	$\begin{array}{r} 3\ 1\ 7\ 6\ 5 \\ -\ 1\ 8\ 9\ 9\ 9 \\ \hline £1\ 2\ 7\ 6\ 6 \end{array}$		1 (5C8b)
5	0.783, 0.82, 0.824, 1.02, 1.1		1 (5F8)
6	The analogue clock shows 4.05 pm. The digital clock shows 15:57 = 3.57 pm. So the digital clock is **8 minutes slow.**		1 (4M4b)
7	E.g.		1 (5M7b/ 6M7a)
8	Two trumpets are 192 ÷ 2 = 96 cm long. So, the clarinet is 155 – 96 = **59 cm**.	2 marks for the correct answer, otherwise 1 mark for a correct method.	2 (5M9b)
9	6.3 km = 6.3 × 1000 = 6300 m 63 ÷ 7 = 9, so 6300 ÷ 7 = 9 × 100 = 900 So Juan walks **900 m** each day.	2 marks for the correct answer, otherwise 1 mark for a correct method.	2 (5M5/ 5C7b)
10	E.g.		2 (3F2)
11	Cost = £5.50 × 20 + £50 £5.50 × 20 = £5.50 × 10 × 2 = £55 × 2 = £110 £110 + £50 = **£160**		1 (6A2)
12	$\frac{2}{5} = \frac{4}{10}$ and $1\frac{1}{10} = \frac{11}{10}$ So $1\frac{1}{10} - \frac{2}{5} = \frac{11}{10} - \frac{4}{10} = \frac{7}{10}$ So $\frac{2}{5} + \frac{7}{10} = 1\frac{1}{10}$		1 (5F2a/ 5F4)
13	1.598 and 0.402		1 (5F8)
14	The temperature in the bedroom is 25 °C. The temperature in the garden is -5 °C. You add 5 °C to go from –5 °C to 0 °C, and then add 25 °C to get to 25 °C. So the difference between the two temperatures is 5 °C + 25 °C = 30 °C. 30 °C ÷ 2 = 15 °C, so halfway between the temperatures is 15 °C below 25 °C. So the temperature in the garage is 25 °C – 15 °C = **10 °C.**	2 marks for the correct answer, otherwise 1 mark for reading both thermometers correctly, or for a correct method.	2 (6N5)
15	2 marks for the correct answers in all three boxes, otherwise 1 mark for correct answers in two boxes.		2 (5C5a)
16	(0, 0), (1, -1) and (2, 0)	2 marks for all three correct coordinates, otherwise 1 mark for two correct coordinates.	2 (6P3)
17	12 large buckets fill a 60 litre tub, so 3 large buckets contain 60 ÷ 4 = 15 litres of water. This means that 5 small buckets contain 15 litres of water, so one small bucket holds 15 ÷ 5 = **3 litres**.	2 marks for the correct answer, otherwise 1 mark for a correct method.	2 (6R4)
18	375 – 7 = 368 $\begin{array}{r} 2\ 3 \\ 1\ 6\ \overline{)3\ 6\ 8} \\ -\ 3\ 2 \\ \hline 4\ 8 \\ -\ 4\ 8 \\ \hline 0 \end{array}$ So, each child takes **23** raisins.	2 marks for the correct answer, otherwise 1 mark for a long division with no more than one error.	2 (6C8)
19a	The apple sector is $\frac{1}{4}$ of the pie chart. $\frac{1}{2}$ of 300 = 150, so $\frac{1}{4}$ of 300 = 150 ÷ 2 = **75**		1 (6S1)
19b	The cherry segment is 60°. So the fraction that were cherry tarts is $\frac{60}{360} = \frac{6}{36} = \frac{1}{6}$.		1 (6S1)
20	The grey triangle is isosceles, so the other base angle is 65°, and the third angle in the triangle is 180° – 65° – 65° = 50°. Angle a is vertically opposite this angle, so a = **50°**.	2 marks for the correct answer, otherwise 1 mark for a correct method.	2 (6G4a/ 6G4b)

KS2 Maths — Answers & Mark Scheme

1224 - 30304

© CGP 2020

Set B – Answers

Qu.	Answer	Marking notes	Marks (Domain)
21	$\begin{array}{r} 1\ 7 \\ 6\overline{)1\ 0\ ^4 2} \end{array}$ So, Juan needs 17 packs of stamps. To find 3.30 × 17, work out 33 × 17, then divide by 10. $\begin{array}{r} 3\ ^3 3 \\ \times\ 1\ 7 \\ \hline 2\ 3\ ^2 1 \\ 3\ 3\ 0 \\ \hline 5\ 6\ 1 \end{array}$ 561 ÷ 10 = 56.1, so £3.30 × 17 = £56.10. So, Juan gets 3 × £20 – £56.10 = **£3.90** change.	3 marks for the correct answer. Otherwise, 2 marks for a correct method with no more than one error. 1 mark for a correct method with more than one error.	3 (5M9a/ 5C8a)

Set B Paper 3

Qu.	Answer	Marking notes	Marks (Domain)
1a	3690		1 (4N4b)
1b	12 000		1 (4N4b)
2a	6:30 pm = 18:30 13 minutes before 18:30 = **18:17**.		1 (3M4f/ 4M4b)
2b	Two hours on from 6.30 pm is 8.30 pm. 9.12 pm is 30 + 10 + 2 minutes = 42 minutes on from 8.30 pm, so the play is **2** hours and **42** minutes long.		1 (3M4f/ 4M4b)
3a	Morning: $20 + 20 + \frac{3}{4} \times 20$ = 20 + 20 + 15 = 55 cups Afternoon: $20 + \frac{1}{4} \times 20$ = 20 + 5 = 25 cups Evening: $20 + 20 + \frac{1}{2} \times 20$ = 20 + 20 + 10 = 50 cups So total = 55 + 25 + 50 = **130**.		1 (4S2)
3b	50 – 25 = **25**		1 (4S2)
4	Two hundred thousand		1 (6N3)
5a	22° (accept any angle between 20° and 24°).		1 (5G4c)
5b	Right-angled		1 (4G2a)
6	The area of the room is 6 × 8 = 48 m². $\begin{array}{r} 4\ 8 \\ \times\ \ \ 4 \\ \hline 1\ 9\ 2 \\ \ \ ^3\ \end{array}$ So, the carpet will cost **£192**.	2 marks for the correct answer, otherwise 1 mark for a correct method.	2 (5M7b/ 4C8)
7	⑤ ⑦ ② × ③ ① ⑦ ① ⑥	2 marks for all three digits correct, otherwise 1 mark for 2 digits correct.	2 (4C7)

Qu.	Answer	Marking notes	Marks (Domain)
8	The left-hand vertical side of the shape is 5 + 4 = 9 cm long. So, the perimeter is 4 + 4 + 7 + 5 + 11 + 9 = **40 cm**.		1 (5M7a)
9	101 ÷ 1000 = **0.101**		1 (5C6b/ 6F6)
10	Half of £2.40 is £1.20. 6 × £1.20 = £7.20 So the total price is £7.20 + £2.40 = **£9.60**.	2 marks for the correct answer, otherwise 1 mark for a correct method.	2 (5M9a/ 5C8a)
11	Each piece of chocolate weighs 72 g ÷ 12 = 6 g. 5 × 6 g = 30 g, so there is 72 g – 30 g = **42 g** remaining.	2 marks for the correct answer, otherwise 1 mark for a correct method.	2 (6R1)
12	$\frac{1}{5}$ = 0.2, and 0.2 + 0.3 = 0.5. So $\frac{1}{5}$ and **0.3** should be circled.		1 (6F11)
13	Volume of carton = 5 × 9 × 10 = 450 cm³. 450 ÷ 150 = 45 ÷ 15 = 3, so it takes Billy **3** days to drink the carton.	2 marks for the correct answer, otherwise 1 mark for a correct method.	2 (6M8a/ 5M9c)
14a	E.g. 99 × 101 is the same as 99 × 100 + 99.		1 (6C8)
14b	9999		1 (6C8)
15	10% of 50 = 5, so 40% of 50 = 5 × 4 = 20. So, there are 50 – 20 – 18 = 12 brown fish. So $\frac{12}{50}$ (or $\frac{6}{25}$) of the fish are brown.	2 marks for the correct answer, otherwise 1 mark for a correct method.	2 (6R2/ 6F11)
16a	20 + 10 = 30 30 ÷ 6 = **5**		1 (5C8b)
16b	1 × 6 – 10 = 6 – 10 = –4, so he rolled a **1**.		1 (5C8b)
17	7		1 (6C5)
18a	Q = 10P + 3		1 (6A2)
18b	E.g. P = 1, Q = 13 P = 2, Q = 23		1 (6A4)
19	$\begin{array}{r} 3\ .\ 6\ 0 \\ +\ 4\ .\ 7\ 5 \\ \hline 8\ .\ 3\ 5 \\ {}^1\ \end{array}$ $\frac{4}{5}$ of the bag is left, so $\frac{1}{5}$ of the bag of compost is 8.35 kg. $\begin{array}{r} 8\ .\ 3\ 5 \\ \times\ \ \ \ \ 5 \\ \hline 4\ 1\ .\ 7\ 5 \\ {}^1\ \ ^2\ \end{array}$ So there were **41.75 kg** of compost in the bag to start with.	2 marks for the correct answer, otherwise 1 mark for a correct method.	2 (5F10)
20a	Diameter = 3 × 2 = **6**		1 (6G5)
20b	The horizontal line between P and (7, 5) goes through the centre of the circle, so it is a diameter. So, the x coordinate of P is 7 – 6 = 1. The y coordinate is the same as for the point (7, 5). So, P = **(1, 5)**.		1 (6P3)

MHP26U